THE COURAGE
OF A
CONSERVATIVE

JAMES G. WATT
WITH DOUG WEAD

SIMON AND SCHUSTER / NEW YORK

PUBLISHED BY SIMON AND SCHUSTER

A DIVISION OF SIMON & SCHUSTER, INC.

SIMON & SCHUSTER BUILDING

ROCKEFELLER CENTER

1230 AVENUE OF THE AMERICAS

NEW YORK, NEW YORK 10020

SIMON AND SCHUSTER AND COLOPHON ARE REGISTERED

TRADEMARKS OF SIMON & SCHUSTER, INC.

DESIGNED BY JENNIE NICHOLS/LEVAVI & LEVAVI

MANUFACTURED IN THE UNITED STATES OF AMERICA

1 3 5 7 9 10 8 6 4 2

LIBRARY OF CONGRESS CATALOGING-IN-PUBLICATION DATA

WATT, JAMES G., DATE–

THE COURAGE OF A CONSERVATIVE.

BIBLIOGRAPHY: P.

INCLUDES INDEX.

I. CONSERVATISM—UNITED STATES. 2. UNITED STATES—

POLITICS AND GOVERNMENT—1981– . I. WEAD, DOUG.

II. TITLE.

JA84.U5W35 1985   320.5'2'0973   85-18268

ISBN: 0-671-52835-1

NOTES OF ACKNOWLEDGMENT

One of the fascinating aspects of serving in public office was the people I met in the course of duty. Doug Wead's name appeared in several letters of introduction long before we were to meet. When the hour came, we had an instant rapport.

Because of our shared heritage and desire to change the course of America, a close bond of friendship was established. It was at Doug Wead's insistence and by the utilization of his skills that this book was begun.

There came moments when encouragement from my devoted wife, Leilani, challenged me to reach levels of creativity and perseverance that were needed to continue.

Here also belong grateful acknowledgments to Mary Achor and Barbara Hodel, who enthusiastically edited the manuscript and became convinced of the worth of the message. I want to thank Simon & Schuster and, in particular, my editor, Bob Asahina, who chose to publish *The Courage of a Conservative*.

To those few
who have the courage
to make a difference.

CONTENTS

PART III

EPILOGUE

INTRODUCTION

The Courage of a Conservative has been an interesting book to write. It is not a revisionist history of my service in government; it is not an attack on the media and their lack of professional integrity; nor is it a strategy for "victory" with all the answers.

It is a book calling for change so we can greet the twenty-first century with the same enthusiasm that freedom and liberty brought to other periods of America's past. It is about what the modern conservative movement must do in order to give the nation the leadership that is so sorely needed.

The background reaches no further into history than the early 1960s, with President John Kennedy and Senator Barry Goldwater, then the Vietnam War and Watergate. Those benchmarks are the "decision points" in the contemporary political era that have influenced the public and the direction of America.

Who are the leaders who have the courage to bring about the changes that are needed?

Must one point out that from ancient times a decline in courage has been considered the beginning of the end?

—ALEXANDER SOLZHENITSYN

PART

I

THE BATTLE
FOR AMERICA

CHAPTER

1

There is an intense battle raging in this land. It can be described in political terms, theological expressions or economic equations because it is being fought in the halls of government, in the churches and in the marketplace. Its outcome will determine how we and our children will be governed in the twenty-first century.

The focus of the battle has become the dignity of the individual versus the domination of government. Will America have a society of giant bureaucratic institutions, in both the public and the private sector, institutions that will have increasing power to control the economic and social behavior of the individual? Or will we have a society that restores and respects the dignity of individuals, so that they can enjoy their spiritual freedom and political liberty?

Since its beginnings in the early 1960s, the modern conservative movement has been warning the American people that we are at a crossroads. A massive, powerful government bureaucracy egged on by selfish special-interest groups is encroaching on the rights of the individual.

The threats to our government, an experiment that commenced with the American Revolution of the 1770s, have a chilling similarity to events following more recent revolutions in other lands. Leaders in other countries have risen up to champion liberty and freedom, only to see the results of their blood and sacrifice lost through institutionalization of power. In place of their dreams stand ugly totalitarian states with centralized bureaucracies or even dictators squeezing the life out of their very own citizens.

Until now, the American experiment has shown amazing resilience. All around us, revolutions have come and gone, while, somehow, our purpose has survived. But the first signs of the erosion of liberty are all around us, even though they are discounted by some without much alarm.

The loss of individual liberty has usually begun by laws created, with the best of intentions, "in the name of the people" and for "the collective good." These are beguiling arguments—some people find them irresistible. "The world is not as simple as it was in the days of Washington or Lincoln," they tell us. "Some compromises may be necessary to address the problems of a modern age." But what has not changed is human nature, and what people will do with corrupting power when they have it.

As we look to the twenty-first century, America must make significant changes in the role and performance of government if we are to protect spiritual freedom, political liberty and the dignity of the individual. We conservatives must demonstrate the courage to face the challenge and to forge the changes. It will not be easy, but neither was the first step. When Thomas Jefferson declared independence from excessive government, he wrote, "For the support of this Declaration, with a firm reliance on the protection of divine Providence, we mutually pledge to each other our lives, our fortunes, and our sacred honor."

There is time to bring about change, and therefore, there is hope. Ironically, our best hope lies in the fact that our freedom has been eroding just long enough for us to have a record to study. We can begin to see where we are headed by taking a look at the winding trail behind us.

THE AMERICAN EXPERIMENT

While serving as secretary of the interior, I received a special invitation for dinner in the private quarters of the White House. President and Mrs. Reagan were gracious hosts. After dinner, they gave my wife, Leilani, and me a tour with an account of some of the interesting events that had unfolded in those private rooms. It was a moving experience for us. We were just two ordinary people from Wyoming, yet we were a part of the nation's present, reviewing a bit of her past.

We stopped in the yellow Oval Room where, on New Year's Day in 1801, John Adams had entertained the first guests of the White House. Looking out through the south windows, I was captivated by the beautiful, lighted panorama.

Struck by the symbolism of our great monuments, I realized it was not the men we immortalized but rather the principles they personified. There, directly in front of us was the towering Washington Monument, a daily reminder to all of us of the integrity and honesty of George Washington, our founding father.

Washington had the personal courage to stand against the oppressive government of England, which wanted to tax individual Americans without regard for their concerns. This monument boldly stands as a symbol of the courage and strength that must be exercised to maintain the integrity of a free society.

Beyond it was the memorial to Thomas Jefferson, the champion of liberty and the author of the Declaration of Independence, which states that "all Men are created equal, that they are endowed by their Creator with certain inalienable Rights, that among these are Life, Liberty and the Pursuit of Happiness."

Written on the memorial walls are passages expressing Jefferson's recognition of God as the source of human rights and liberties. Jefferson challenged the king of England and the Tories on behalf of the dignity of men and women. He contended that each person had certain rights above those of government, and he was willing to pay the price for those rights in battle.

As I looked to the right, I saw the Lincoln Memorial, a reminder that freedom is not free. Its price is a constant struggle against oppressive governments. For the first hundred years of our history as a nation, some Americans were slaves with no rights or liberties at all. The next hundred years, even with the abolition of slavery, were not proud ones for America. The Lincoln Memorial is a warning. If even the descendants of persecuted and freedom-seeking immigrants could rationalize slavery, then we must never be complacent about the uses to which power will be put by governments. If we forfeit power to our enemies or to our own institutions of government, then we must be prepared to be their slaves.

It is a bloody monument, this memorial to Lincoln. A half million young men died in the Civil War, ten times the number of American casualties in the Vietnam War, whose memorial is laid out in a slope of grass a few yards away. The process of making slaves was not nearly so messy or bloody as the process of making men free. It is an easy thing to lose one's freedom, and a terrible struggle to gain it back.

These three memorials, the Washington, Jefferson and the Lincoln, symbolize the fundamental ideals of America. Washington's battle was a physical war to secure the integrity of the peoples of the colonies, so that life might be given to the newly declared country. Jefferson's battle was an intellectual struggle formulating the concepts and principles that would justify and preserve the God-given liberty of men and women so that their lives would have meaning and dignity. Lincoln's battle was a political conflict as well as a war to resolve whether our nation could continue to exist half slave and half free. Freedom was the result. The memorials represent the fundamental ideals of our nation: integrity, liberty and freedom.

As I turned to look in the other direction, I was impressed with the beauty and grandeur of the nation's Capitol, with its glowing white dome where our representatives and senators gather to debate the public policy that will govern this nation. They represent the diversity of the American people. We are Jews, we are Christians, we are whatever religion we want to be—or even none at all. We are black, white, red, brown and yellow, urban and rural, poor and rich. We are pluralistic, championing individualism. This is our strength.

THE RIGHTS OF THE INDIVIDUAL

During the almost three years I served the country as a member of the president's cabinet, my love for America grew deeply. Leilani and I visited forty-three of our fifty states. As secretary of the interior, I was able to see firsthand the beauty, grandeur and majesty of America. We were able to walk in many of the national parks, the "crown jewels" of this land. We visited the wildlife refuges. We toured the farm belt, which can feed the world. We surveyed the industrial states, which give us our high standard of living. We walked the beautiful coastal areas, the magnificent plains, the towering mountains, the lush valleys, the colorful deserts and the mighty forests. To see this land in all of its dimensions is inspiring.

As we flew, drove, boated, hiked and walked across the country, I pondered the question, "What makes America great?" The answer was evident everywhere. The greatness of our nation is not her natural resources. It is her people.

How have we, the American people, made our country greater than all others? Is it our free-enterprise system, which some say has triumphed so convincingly over the worldwide Socialist experiment? No. Immigrants were coming here long before America was rich or powerful. It was not the guarantee of riches that brought them. It was the guarantee of opportunity. They didn't want a handout, or even a hand. They simply wanted a chance.

A chance to do what? Economic opportunity was not the reason the Pilgrims came to Massachusetts or the Catholics to Maryland or the Quakers to Pennsylvania. They were seeking personal liberty and spiritual freedom. They were fleeing excessive government that in the name of "public good" was oppressing those with minority opinions.

From the perspective of European history, a good Catholic king was not considered oppressive for chasing down those last unrepentant Protestant rebels or for censoring publishers and controlling the press. He was "saving people from hell." In another country, his Protestant counterpart would execute Catholics, all in the name of the people. "Defender of the Faith" was the favorite title of the English monarch. There was always a respectable-sounding theological and moral rationale for oppression. The same is true today. It is not out of "meanness" that the Soviet Union prohibits religious worship for its youth, or imprisons such great philosophers and writers as Alexander Solzhenitsyn when they try to write about their faith or engage in political debate. It is "for the good of the state." It is even to "protect" the individual from himself.

Those early immigrants who came in such numbers to America were not fleeing governments that oppressed their people; rather, they were fleeing governments that oppressed their minorities. The Puritans and minority Catholics came from England; the Protestant Huguenots came from France. During the potato famine, the starving and harassed Irish, who had become a minority in the British Empire, fled their own land. The Jews came from czarist Russia and Nazi Germany. The peasants of Russia came when they were told that they must serve the czar in the name of God and accept their position in life. Now some of Russia's finest artists, writers, ballet dancers and scientists seek asylum from a government that talks about a "classless society" and periodically harasses them for "seeking egotistical satisfaction at the expense of the masses."

So if the lure of America has not been just her wealth, is it the spiritual and philosophical freedom? No. Spiritual freedom alone cannot be the explanation. If English Catholics only wanted the chance to be Catholics, they could have gone to Spain and joined the majority there.

The combination of spiritual freedom and individual liberty was the reason. Catholics did not come to America because it was Catholic. Jews did not come because it was Jewish. Intellectuals did not come because it was intellectual. Peasants did not come because it was a peasant society. These immigrants chose America because of its unique promise that not only they but others could be free as well—the pluralistic ideal. They had grown frightened with the whole idea of powerful centralized government. They had been on the receiving end of it, so they had grown to detest it and despise its hypocrisy, even when it offered to champion their race or religion or creed. It was the idea of a limited government with many checks and balances that appealed to immigrants—a system offering the hope that it would not only tolerate them now, but tolerate them tomorrow as well.

The motivation of those immigrants to the United States is the same motivation of conservatives today. It is the concern for the individual and his or her dignity. It is not a new concern. History tells us that mankind has always had a yearning for liberty that flows like a stream of life. From it comes the cry for the right of men and women to assemble together, to establish their own government, to work for whom they desire, to train their children as they wish, to provide for their own, to exercise their political liberty.

The individual frequently has found himself trapped by the will of government. Often it has been for the noblest of reasons that political liberty has been denied the individual. Sometimes the force of oppression was called the king, sometimes a dictator or warlord or czar, sometimes it was the Gestapo. But always it was excessive government.

The same history tells yet another story. Mankind has also had a yearning for another kind of freedom that also flows like a stream. That yearning is the desire to worship God, to join with others of like, precious faith, to develop their own doctrines and to train and educate their own children, to enjoy spiritual freedom. It is hard for twentieth-century youth reared in our now secularized society to appreciate how deeply rooted Western science, art and politics have been in religious faith. But history very clearly shows us how desperate the desire has been for spiritual freedom and how the struggle for it, too, has always been opposed by excessive government.

At one point in history, destiny provided that these two streams of life, political liberty and spiritual freedom, would come together in a mighty confluence called America. This combination, which permits pluralism, has made America great. It is these principles that still attract modern pilgrims like Alexander Solzhenitsyn. And it is the erosion of these principles that threatens our uniqueness.

Washington understood this. We are not some special race. We are English, Scandinavian, German, Indian, Latin, Asian, African. We are not culturally or artistically superior to any other people. It is the principles that have limited the role of government that have enabled us to be great.

That is why Washington refused another term as president. He knew that the American people, and he himself, were not above yielding to the temptations of power to oppress others. If our first president, famous for his integrity, was so frightened of governmental power, how can we be so eager to employ it as the solution to every problem?

A LIMITED ROLE FOR GOVERNMENT

Then what is the conservative alternative? If government cannot solve all the problems of the people, who will? Shall we let the disadvantaged starve? Shall we allow confidence men to promote phony cures for cancer? Should all federal regulations be cut, all subsidies to the needy stopped? Should the federal government pull out and leave volunteer organizations, the states and local communities holding the bag for everything? Shall we return to the separatism of colonial America?

Of course not. Modern conservatives recognize that circumstances are different today from what they were in the 1770s. We would not repeal the Social Security system or eliminate welfare payments to the truly needy. We acknowledge that a kind of second revolution took place when, under Franklin Roosevelt, the federal government stepped in and took charge during the emergency of the Great Depression. We applaud the ability of a centralized government to respond quickly in a modern age when national problems arise. We applaud the federal government's role in helping to check racial discrimination, for example.

That is why I refer to our movement as the *modern* conservative movement. In America's past, we conservatives of today would hardly be considered conservative at all. We are conservative now about the degree of federal involvement. At best, we see excessive government as promoting a failed economic policy, financially defrauding the very disadvantaged people it had promised to help. At worst, we see excessive government as a threat to the spiritual freedom and individual liberty of its citizens.

Modern conservatives have not called for the dismantling of the entire government bureaucracy. But we have called for a serious pruning, and, far beyond any technical adjustment here or there, we are seeking to recapture the original American idea.

The modern conservative takes issue with the suggestion that the American system is flawed or corrupt and requires massive governmental intervention to right it. We have no romantic illusions about a worldwide Socialist movement that manifests itself in its newly formed governments with mass murders of millions, and in its older established governments with inefficient industry, creating products that don't work and shortages for its workers. Conservatives feel no compulsion to borrow economic solutions from countries that can't even supply their own people with basic needs. We believe in the original American idea of guaranteeing dignity for the individual through political liberty and spiritual freedom. We seek a counterrevolution to recapture the best of that idea.

A QUESTION OF SURVIVAL

America is at a crossroads. With each election, she is taking another step. We conservatives argue that her roots are good, that we can trust and should conserve the original idea. There is no other country with our spiritual freedom and individual liberty. Let the Swedes nationalize their banks to resolve a temporary economic crisis. Let the French government experiment with socialism and take ownership of its steel factories. Let the British tax their corporations at an 80 percent rate and socialize their medicine. Let the Cubans and Nicaraguans protect their peoples from the "evils of religion" and use government to fight—and, in the case of the Cubans, actually close—their churches and synagogues.

America is one of a kind. She should not be insecure and should not let her imperfections panic her into mimicking inferior models.

There was another special moment during that private dinner at the White House. Before the evening was over, we stopped in a narrow hall. President Reagan nodded solemnly toward a browned, frayed parchment framed on the wall. "Let me show you this, Jim," he said. "This is an original of the national anthem. It's in Francis Scott Key's own handwriting."

We chatted a moment about the history of "The Star-Spangled

Banner," and then I told the president this story. A few years ago, I was attending an evening church service. Our pastor asked us to stand and sing the national anthem. As I stood with the congregation, I heard for probably the first time the meaning of the words I had sung so many times. As I came to the end of the first verse, I sang with gusto these words: "Oh, say does that Star-Spangled Banner yet wave / O'er the land of the free and the home of the brave?" Our national anthem ends with a question mark. I had never noticed it before. It is a question that must be answered, and answered again and again.

President Reagan was deeply moved by my story, and as I finished, his eyes misted. Neither of us said anything. Outside, on the South Lawn of the White House, illuminated by bright spotlights, the American flag was billowing in the wind. Over what kind of land is our flag waving? Is it a land of people who are free to exercise independent choice, or has their grip on freedom begun to slip? Is it waving over the home of people who are brave enough to face an unknown future without guarantees from the government? Brave enough to resist a foreign power whose weapons could hold the whole world hostage if it threatened to destroy mankind? Francis Scott Key's question must be answered for itself by each generation.

CHOOSING SIDES

CHAPTER

2

When I write about liberals and conservatives, I am writing about distinct political philosophies. They both have consistent themes. They offer a clear choice and opposite directions for America's future.

There are some who would disagree with this description. There are moderates who pick and choose from both sides in this argument. They are offended by both liberals and conservatives. They would view as alarmist the rhetoric they occasionally hear from both sides about the threat to America's future.

Moderates believe the two sides have evolved haphazardly, with cultural and social factors having as much influence as politics. While they admit to occasional philosophical consistency among a liberal's ideas or a conservative's ideas, they tend to think of the two sides as the Red Team and the Blue Team. To moderates, it doesn't really matter who wins—neither side is good or bad.

To make their case, moderates will often point out the inconsistencies of the advocates. They will say to the one, "How can you claim to be conservative when you support government subsidies for bailing out big business?" And to the other, "How can you claim to be liberal when without compassion or fairness you ignore the plight of the American Indian?"

But there are definite liberal and conservative philosophies on how we should be governed. If no consistent conservative or liberal philosophy existed, or if it were so complex that the layman couldn't immediately see it, then how could a moderate spot a conservative or liberal inconsistency?

You will notice that I am not yet arguing about why I believe we conservatives are right. I am only saying that the two sides exist. They are distinct, and, though their historical evolution is sometimes confusing, twisting like a riverbed here or there and sometimes even circling back, conservatives and liberals are ultimately flowing in opposite directions. They offer America a choice, and once a decision is fully made, she may not be able to change her mind.

WHO IS RIGHT?

The contest between liberals and conservatives is a moral battle. It is a contest over who is right and who is wrong. There are many liberals who would take exception to this statement. They complain that it smacks too much of religion. They would say we conservatives are always trying to moralize and express issues in terms of good and bad. Still, no matter how they may protest, this is the truth: the battle is over who is right.

When a staunch liberal says he is for the nuclear freeze, it is not because he wants to get elected. He would support the nuclear freeze even if he only got one vote. He believes it is right, that it is a moral outrage to continue to build weapons to blow up the world.

When a true conservative says that a nuclear freeze wouldn't work unless the Russians actually complied with it, he is not just posturing to get into office. He would say the same thing even if it meant losing his seat in the Senate. He would point out the moral difference between the West and the Marxist totalitarian governments, with their history of mass exterminations in Cambodia and China and Russia, and their outrageous use of drugs to alter the minds of their own dissidents. The conservative would be making a moral argument about the need to remain vigilant and to protect the sovereignty of our free nation.

When liberals say they are pro-choice in the abortion debate, they are not simply pulling a cause out of a hat. Liberals would contend that it is immoral for wealthy women to be able to pay for abortions if they want them, while the government does not provide funds for that service to poorer women. Liberals want a woman to have the freedom, regardless of economics, to give or deny birth to a baby as she desires.

Conservatives, on the other hand, want to protect the rights of the unborn baby. It is a clear moral issue. Does society protect the rights of the unborn or the desires of the mother?

Even moderates moralize about their positions. When Barry Goldwater said that moderation in the pursuit of freedom is no virtue, and extremism in the defense of liberty is no vice, he simply stated a truth that any liberal, conservative, Communist or capitalist could easily express to his own constituents. What was offensive to moderates was his use of the word *extremism*. To moderates, it expresses a commitment to a cause beyond the point where they are willing to go.

Moderates would say that a deep commitment, whether liberal or conservative, is itself dangerous. It makes little difference who wins an election or who controls the Senate or the media or the special-interest groups, moderates would say. The circumstances, not a political philosophy, dictate decisions. Therefore, ideologues can be dangerous. Since they are value-oriented, they may adhere to a cause when it is not in the interests of the country to do so, according to a moderate.

Of course, moderates make a good point when they say that circumstances have a bearing on decisions, that some things are going to happen no matter who is in power. But to say that people cannot affect their own destinies is to say that Nazism was inevitable, that the Nazis cannot be blamed for the flow of history. "It was necessary for all that murder to come out; it was unavoidable. It would have happened no matter who had been in power."

That's nonsense. The German people in the 1930s had the ability to make decisions, and they did. Some resisted Nazism and died for it. This is not to say that every German who did not resist Nazism to the death was guilty of every crime committed by his government. Many people may have been sincere and well intentioned. Some may not have really known what was going on. Nevertheless, Nazism triumphed because many people chose it, and that choice was wrong. And it was von Papen and the moderates who allowed Hitler to come to power in 1933.

So Goldwater was quite right when he made the point about extremism. Some would argue that the extremism that led American and British bombers to bomb civilian targets in Germany was absolutely right and necessary. It speeded up the end of the war and saved millions of Jews who were being exterminated in 1944 at the rate of a hundred thousand per month. Certainly, when Harry Truman ordered an atomic bomb dropped on Japan, it was an act of extremism. But many historians would defend his decision. And, of course, life is full of less dramatic and less controversial examples. The point I am making here is that even the argument between moderates and ideologues, liberal or conservative, is a moral argument.

It is quite absurd to say that morality is irrelevant to political philosophy, that government is simply an exercise in accounting, that it is all mathematical. And no matter how popular it may be at the moment, the belief that "policy is dictated by circumstances, it doesn't really matter who is in power" is an attempt to avoid moral responsibility.

CONSERVATIVE OR LIBERAL
ABOUT WHAT?

What do I mean when I say liberal and conservative? There really must be a definition of terms, a point of reference. There must be something about which to be liberal or conservative or moderate.

In recent years, liberals have argued and written as if the point of reference in this whole debate is *whether* to meet the needs of people. This view has been popularized by sympathetic media. It is difficult to watch a sincere and well-intentioned television newsman reciting unemployment figures without feeling some anger toward anyone in government who would hesitate to offer help. The intended implication of this view is that liberals are liberal in responding to the needs of people, moderates are reluctant, and conservatives are selfish and uncaring.

This is absurd. If the needs of people were the point of reference, we wouldn't even be using the terms *liberal* or *moderate* or *conservative*. We would all be "liberals." How could anyone be moderate or reluctant to help poor people or victims of discrimination? What virtue is there in being moderately concerned about people? To be conservative in responding to such need would be unconscionable and cruel. If the needs of people were what this debate were all about, I would be "liberal" in an instant, for I am committed to the dignity, freedom and liberty of the individual. People are the important factor, not institutions or corporations or stone monuments or grassy malls or even what is said in history books.

In the philosophical war between conservatives and liberals, there is a battle over semantics and words and terminology. We are not debating whether to meet the needs of people, or whether there should be discrimination or poverty or peace. Needs are not the point of reference about which we are liberal or conservative. The distorted claim that liberals are the only ones who care about people has been used to defeat the conservative position. Although many Americans have been misled by this argument, they have begun to recognize the deception promoted by evening newscasters who espouse liberal views about "who really cares about the people." When millions upon millions of Americans voted for a conservative candidate, it was not because they weren't concerned, for many are themselves suffering discrimination or facing economic difficulties. They voted precisely because they do care, and they believe the conservative has the best answers to ensure individual liberty and economic prosperity.

Then what is the point of reference? And where do the terms *liberal* and *conservative* come from? The point of reference is *how* to meet the needs of people and the constitutional limitations on the role of government. Liberals will allow for a very liberal interpretation of the Constitution when they believe it will help them meet the needs of the people. They are willing to change the forms of law and government to meet immediate needs. Moderates are much more cautious, and we conservatives can be downright tough and very protective of the constitutional limits on the role of government. We believe that the basic American system has worked well. The constitutional rights of political, religious and economic freedoms have given Americans the highest quality of life in the world. Like the early revolutionary Americans, we conservatives fear that self-righteous, unlimited government, no matter how well intentioned, will eventually abuse its powers and everyone's freedom. We conservatives consider ourselves the champions of individual liberty in the battle against the centralization of power.

To be sure, we conservatives can be quite generous when it comes to financing the responsibilities that the Constitution clearly allows. After great debate, our founding fathers determined that a national army was necessary to "provide for the common defense." We are big supporters of a strong America. Yet we conservatives can be very cautious about other, more recent, government responsibilities that had been considered unconstitutional for nearly two centuries but in recent years have

been determined by liberal Congresses and courts to be legitimate.
Whenever possible, conservatives will seek to restrain government
power, or at least direct it in such a way that it will involve the
private sector and give people incentives to deal with their own
problems in order to protect their traditional values, individual
dignity and freedom.

So the point of reference is the role of government in meeting
the needs of people. That—and not who has the most compassion—is the subject of the debate.

Both moderates and liberals determine policy on the basis of
the perceived situation, the immediate need. They are willing
to compromise the traditional restraints of the American system
if it will satisfactorily address the need at hand. Conservatives,
on the other hand, look to values and absolutes to direct them.

There is a theological parallel to this political debate. Conservative politicians attract conservative theologians precisely because both look to traditional values and absolutes for direction.
Some scholars suggest that the political and the religious share
the same absolutes and values. It is true that the structure of
American government borrows much from its Judeo-Christian
tradition.

There is a similar parallel with liberals. Modern liberal theologians who have come to question the absolutes of their own
faith have much in common with modern political liberals who
have become quite critical and self-conscious of the hypocritical
role they believe that America plays in the world. Both groups
would view themselves as iconoclastic, even daring, in their willingness to defy tradition. They say, "Tell me the problem. Don't
tell me the rules." It is situational ethics for liberals in either case.

THE DEBATE MOVES LEFT

With each decade the debate about the role of government has
become increasingly liberal because of the power of the liberal
Establishment, the Congress, big business, the unions and the
media, all of which I will discuss in the next chapter.

Of course, some people would not accept this assessment. They would say that there has been a shift to the Right among the general population. Surveys do show more and more voters identifying themselves as conservatives. But that is not so much because the voters are moving Right as it is because the debate is moving Left. As the liberal leaders become more and more liberal, they are leaving more and more people behind them. Some people have become conservative by default. They just won't move any farther Left.

A case could be made that we conservatives of today are so liberal by yesterday's standards that a New Dealer would feel quite at home with us. The big debate twenty-five years ago concerned federal aid to education and whether it would lead to federal controls. Today, by contrast, we are debating whether nine-year-olds violate federal law when they pray over their lunches in a school cafeteria, or whether homosexual teachers have the right to advocate their life-style to their students. Forty-five years ago, liberals contended that federal welfare was desirable for the truly needy and could serve as a transitional support to help capable but temporarily unlucky workers back into the work force. This is exactly the philosophy that we modern conservatives would subscribe to today. But what is the welfare system like now? And when it comes to the contemporary problem of criminal justice, a Harvard professor recently said it best. "There are no more liberals on the crime and law-and-order issue . . . they've all been mugged."[1]

So when I write about conservatives, remember I am writing about modern conservatives. We are probably the most liberal conservatives the nation has ever known. In the context of American history, some would not call us very conservative at all. That is probably why there are now so very many of us. We are warning that today's liberal is threatening to denigrate the dignity of the individual and further erode our spiritual freedom and political liberty. We are no longer debating options within the parameters of the American system. We are, in fact, debating that very system itself.

THE LIBERAL
ESTABLISHMENT

CHAPTER

3

There is one last point I need to make before getting into the fight: the liberals are in power. They are the Establishment. Whether one is talking about labor, education, business, the media, the arts or even government bureaucracy, liberalism reigns. Therefore, the burden of this battle is on conservative shoulders. We are the ones calling for change. Since much of its program has become law, the liberal Establishment need do nothing but hang on in order to prevail.

To make my point, let me give you a quick tour of the large voter blocs in this country. The liberals will readily claim many of them, despite recent Republican victories. For example, liberals control the National Education Association and the leadership of the nation's largest union, the AFL-CIO. Liberalism reigns at the National Council of Churches. And the leadership of many minority groups, including blacks and Hispanics, are liberal.

Still, we conservatives are waging a fierce battle for the loyalty of the Hispanics because we believe we have the most to offer for their future. We also claim that blacks have been betrayed by liberal politicians and policies and will thus be prime candidates for recruitment in the next decade. But the process of identifying who is liberal and who is conservative can be very tricky. The battle for America sometimes takes the form of an ideological guerrilla war. Sometimes the soldiers are most effective when their identities are unknown. It can be frustrating to determine what a newspaper or special-interest group or politician is really up to. It is a sad commentary on our times—but it is most definitely a fact—that the polarization among Americans has become so great that some people find it necessary to deceive others in order to achieve their political ends. The most unfair of all (and, unfortunately, sometimes the most effective) are those voices that self-righteously claim objectivity, but in fact have a rigid ideological agenda.

THOSE SPECIAL-INTEREST GROUPS

Some of the most powerful establishments in American political life are what we have come to call "the special-interest groups." America has always known special interests seeking favor and privilege. We have known of cases in which the railroads, stockmen, labor unions, banks, utilities, environmentalists or other groups had their way. But today there is a new twist. The special-interest groups themselves are now being used as weapons in the great philosophical/political battle between liberals and conservatives. Sometimes the very "cause" or purpose of an organization is subordinated to this fight. Instead of truly working for "peace" or "women's rights" or "the environment," groups are suddenly fighting against liberals or conservatives. But the liberals have been more successful at this strategy than we conservatives have been.

Take, for example, the women's movement, which in some

ways sprang from my own home state of Wyoming, the Equality State, where women were first allowed to vote. There has been, and still is, discrimination against women. Special-interest groups of all types have been created to eliminate this offensive practice. I know of no one in political life who would condone it. In the 1970s, the National Organization for Women came to prominence as the spokesperson for women's rights. Immediately, conservatives charged that NOW was dominated by liberals and that the leadership was leaving little room for women with a more conservative or traditional value orientation. Instead of fighting for all women, regardless of their political views, NOW was exclusively taking up the liberal banner, even if that meant opposing other women.

Of course, there was a very good rationale for this activity. Simply put, the leaders of NOW believed that the liberal movement did more for women than the conservative movement did. They still believe it. For example, in recent years, most of the leaders of NOW have gone on record favoring the nuclear freeze. It is simply madness, they would say, to keep building more and more weapons. A nuclear war is not in the interests of women.

On the face of it, this is a ridiculous argument. A nuclear war would not be any better for men than it would be for women. For that matter, a nuclear war would not be in the best interests of labor, blacks, the environment, children, members of the National Rifle Association or anybody else. Is NOW implying that conservatives want nuclear war?

You see, we are right back to the same old liberal/conservative argument. Of course, the question of nuclear weapons is extremely critical. It is far more important than the question of whether women are getting equal pay with men or whether they are being discriminated against in other ways in our society. But if NOW is going to debate a nuclear freeze or all of the other conservative/liberal arguments, who is going to fight for the rights of women?

What if a woman demanded that women should have equal

pay for equal work, but opposed the Equal Rights Amendment, and believed that it is naive for us to freeze all nuclear weapons unless the Russians do the same? What if she were morally offended by abortion and opposed the use of government tax dollars to support it? Would that woman be endorsed by NOW if she ran for the Senate?

Well, that woman is Paula Hawkins. She ran for the Senate seat from Florida, and not only was the answer to those questions no, she was, in fact, quite vigorously opposed by NOW. (Even so, she won.) At this writing, NOW opposes the only two women serving in the United States Senate. Of sixty women seeking congressional seats in 1984, NOW only supported twenty-three. When President Reagan appointed the third woman member of his cabinet, a momentous occasion that marked the greatest number of women ever to have served in a presidential cabinet in American history, NOW said nothing. It continued to portray the Reagan administration as antiwomen.

On August 19, 1981, President Reagan nominated Sandra Day O'Connor as the first woman in American history to serve on the Supreme Court. It was a lifetime position that could have incalculable legal impact on the role of women in our society. It was the highest governmental position for any woman to have reached in the history of our republic.

All of this is not to say that it is wrong for liberals to use NOW to promote their own cause, only that it is deceptive. NOW is not just a women's organization, but rather an organization promoting the liberal agenda. I am offering a little warning that you must be alert. To assume that all special-interest groups are simply promoting their own causes is naive. In many instances, they seek a strong centralized bureaucracy in order to secure a privileged position for their causes.

Well, you say, conservatives have their own special interest groups, too—such as the National Rifle Association. But that is a good example of the problem we conservatives have in taking on the Establishment. Yes, conservatives are strong constitution-

alists who defend the Bill of Rights and its provision allowing
citizens to bear arms. This was a rigid principle of our founding fathers. Modern conservatives would claim that Poland or
Czechoslovakia or Hungary might never have been tamed by
their Soviet masters if the right to bear arms had existed all along
in Communist totalitarian states. Yes, conservatives will often
vote according to the NRA guidelines. Yes, they will often re-
ceive the support of this powerful lobby. But, no, the NRA is
not a conservative special-interest group. It will not support a
conservative congressman who favors registration of handguns,
even if that congressman passes all the other tests of a good
conservative. The NRA quite consistently represents riflemen,
not conservatives. The National Organization for Women, on
the other hand, frequently opposes women who are not liberal.

One last thing. It may not be wrong for ideologues to seize
control of a cause and use it as a weapon in their own, bigger
war. But it is most definitely wrong for those ideologues to imply
that anyone who is against their greater agenda, liberal or conservative, is also against the cause their special-interest group supposedly represents. For example, it is certainly not antiwomen
for a woman or man to oppose the NOW agenda. Neither is it
antipeace to oppose the programs of the Council for a Liveable
World, nor antienvironment to oppose the extremely liberal
agenda of the paid environmentalists.

For many years the environmental movement championed
great projects and had a healthy impact on legislation. Then,
beginning in the late 1960s, the politicization of the movement
began. By September of 1980, that process was formalized when
the paid leadership of the largest and most active conservation/
environmentalist groups marched lockstep into the Rose Garden
of the White House and endorsed Carter's reelection bid. They
came out in total opposition to Governor Reagan. Again in 1984
they opposed President Reagan.

Today, the statistical evidence of the liberal agenda of this
movement is abundant. Let it suffice for me to say that not one

of these environmental organizations raised a voice in opposition to the 50 percent reduction in appropriations for restoration and improvement of our national parks during the four Carter-Mondale years. Nor did they criticize the liberal members of Congress who voted to cut these funds. When funds for adding new land to the parks system were reduced from $367 million to $65 million in the Carter years, there was only silence from environmentalists. Why? Quite obviously, they had a higher priority than our national park system—the liberal agenda.

And while the liberal leaders of the environmentalist groups never criticized the cut in funding for parks during the Carter administration, they never complimented the Reagan administration for doubling, tripling and quadrupling those funds in its first, second and third years. The restoration and improvement of the national parks system in the 1980s has been spectacular.

Nor did the environmental lobbies applaud the fact that more land was added to the federal estate for park and wildlife purposes in 1983 than in any single year since 1867, when Alaska was purchased from the Russians—which includes the administrations of Teddy Roosevelt, Franklin D. Roosevelt or Jimmy Carter.

Well, you may ask, if all this is true, why didn't you tell us so when you were secretary of the interior? The answer is that I did. I said it every chance I had. But I was not the one who was choosing what you heard or what you saw or what you read during those years.

THE MEDIA

This brings us to one of the most powerful liberal institutions of all, the media. When one quotes Marshall McLuhan's line, "The medium is the message," there is always a ripple of laughter. It doesn't matter if you are speaking to Wall Street investment bankers in tuxedos or husband-and-wife farmers at a picnic somewhere in the Plains states. There is widespread recognition of the fact that the media's power has become enormous, so much so that it may be suicidal for a politician or businessman even to discuss it. McLuhan's line, whatever its original intention, has become a safe way to joke about it, and audiences are always relieved, for they, too, are nervous about that power and are glad to know that they are not alone.

Conservatives say that the majority of the media regularly inject their liberal views right into their news stories. In the past, the media have vociferously denied this and maintained that they were absolutely objective. If they could show a letter of complaint from a liberal, the media would pretend objectivity, saying, "Both sides accuse us of the same thing." But there is much less hypocrisy today. It is becoming more common for members of the media to question their own objectivity. When *Washington Post* editor Ben Bradlee protested at a 1984 newswriters' conference that his paper was not liberal at all, his words prompted a round of laughter from his peers. The consensus was that it is certainly not wrong for a newspaper to be liberal, but it is either hypocritical or deceptive to deny it.

Whether or not the reports we see and hear are politically biased, there can be no debating the fact that most reporters themselves are liberal. In recent years, the press has voted overwhelmingly for the more liberal candidate in presidential elections. The 1980 Rothman-Lichter Survey showed that while the country was going for the Republicans in a landslide, 81 percent of America's journalists were going against the American public and voting for the liberal candidate.[1] The survey went on to determine the views of journalists and editors on a wide range of liberal-conservative issues. In every case, 70 percent to 80 percent of the journalists sided with the liberal argument.

BIG BUSINESS AND THE RICH

All right, you may say, we'll admit that leaders of labor and blacks, the government bureaucracy, the National Council of Churches and other institutions are liberal. And they all use their special-interest groups to advance a liberal agenda. We'll concede the media are liberal, too. But conservatism is the movement of the rich and the big businessman, right? Wrong.

It is true that Franklin Roosevelt's great liberal reforms were opposed by wealthy conservative Republicans. At the time, it was popularly held that wealth and achievement were signs of virtue. The Astors, the Mellons and the Thayers were the American celebrities of their era. They had profited enormously by the free marketplace. Roosevelt's programs smacked of socialism and were vigorously opposed by them. Many Wall Street brokerage firms lost fortunes when governmental regulations were instituted.

The modern conservative movement does indeed applaud the philosophy of individual enterprise and some of the great achievements of those early twentieth-century superwealthy. But modern conservatives would not totally dismantle government. We certainly seek to reform and stabilize the Social Security system, and, though we are calling for more freedom in the marketplace, we would not abolish the Securities and Exchange Commission. We would not return to the days when huge monopolies crowded out the new small businessman. We modern conservatives see ourselves as the champions of small business.

Moreover, those so-called conservative rich Republicans of the early twentieth century were isolationists. Today's conservative movement of the post-1960s, by contrast, is accused of being interventionist and a sucker for any arms procurement legislation that comes along. It is today's liberals who burn their draft cards, reduce defense spending and warn that America can't police the world.

Finally, the greatest distinction of all between conservatives then and now is the fact that the superwealthy of the early twentieth century were protecting the status quo. They were the Establishment. They were America's power brokers, trying to hold their ground in the face of the liberal Roosevelt revolution and the encroaching flood of the labor movement. They lost. Today, the Establishment is liberal. Simply put, the Roosevelt liberal revolution succeeded. It now controls labor, big government, big business, education, the media and many special-interest groups. They rule America.

Conservatives today are not protecting the status quo; they are calling for big changes. They are calling for a counterrevolution, and it is not popular with most of the nervous superwealthy. In the past generation, big business and the rich have suddenly become part of the liberal Establishment. Henry Ford, Sr., may have been horrified by Roosevelt's New Deal, but his grandson has not only made peace with liberals, he has become a bona fide liberal himself. Lee Iacocca of Chrysler is a liberal; so are many other leaders of the nation's largest corporations. The Rockefellers and some other New York bankers may be Republicans, but they are considered so liberal by their own party that all their money hasn't been able to budge convention delegates to pick their man. Jay Rockefeller, West Virginia's former liberal Democratic governor, is said to have raised $150,000 for his reelection bid and then thrown in $12 million of his own money. When he was elected to the United States Senate in 1984, he raised one-and-a-half million dollars and spent another ten million of his personal funds. And what about Harvard, Yale and all those other grand, once-conservative eastern universities that were the favorite charities of the rich and the special preserves of their sons? Well, they are still the favorite charities of the rich, and they are still the special preserves of their sons. Only now they are on the cutting edge of the liberal political movement.

The rich discovered they had a vested interest in a growing centralized bureaucracy. Huge government contracts brought enormous profits to the companies with proper connections. Bureaucratic regulations helped eliminate competition from new businesses. Sometimes government guaranteed their success, bailing out giant corporations that failed, but letting small businesses die by the thousands.

Mostly, the rich have benefited from inflation. Once set in motion, inflation becomes an insidious tool that allows the rich to thrive while it squeezes the life out of the workers and the middle class. During the years of Carter-Mondale, huge fortunes were made by people who were already wealthy. This is not to impugn the motives of Carter-Mondale or any other liberals of the past. That was not what they intended, but that is indeed what happened. Inflation became the poor man's tax.

At this point, even before we have really gotten into the debate, the reader may be tempted to side with the liberal argument. If the liberals are supported by all those special interests, and the giant corporations and superwealthy have become their allies, too, just maybe they are right. But that would mean ignoring the morality of the argument. Just because the liberals are the Establishment doesn't mean they are right, nor does it mean they will always be the Establishment, either.

WHO ARE THE CONSERVATIVES?

The modern conservative movement has come far since liberal Lyndon Johnson trounced conservative Barry Goldwater in 1964. At the time, there were only a few United States senators who would call themselves conservative. Today, there are dozens. Most polls reflect conservative majorities among the general population on specific issues. We even have some of our own newspapers.

In the middle 1960s modern conservatives first started presenting the case that our movement is a populist one. While liberals can always count on union leadership, the rank and file often abandon the liberal candidate in great numbers during an election. The National Council of Churches may always be counted on to embrace the liberal side of any issue, but the members of its various denominations are often offended by the council's ultraleftist activities. The National Organization for Women may be able to count on full media recognition and wide coverage of its annual conventions, but the less publicized Concerned Women for America has two or three times as many members.

In the 1960s, a very small and new National Association of Evangelicals was started. Today, this conservative Christian movement is more vibrant than the rival National Council of Churches. Liberal politicians and news commentators, accustomed to having the church routinely endorse their views, have become alarmed. They refer to this new movement of the religious Right as "dangerous," and they warn that its voter registration drives and publications are "a threat to the democratic process." I say they only threaten the liberals' privileged positions of power.

Most dramatic of all, of course, was the recent reelection of the first self-proclaimed conservative president. In his first term President Reagan had perhaps a year to apply some of the beliefs of modern conservatives before the entrenched liberal congress, bureaucracy and media stopped his counterrevolution short.

But there can be no mistaking the fact that conservative populism has mounted a serious challenge to the liberal Establishment. Liberals are on the defensive now, everywhere. Sometimes their candidates even pose as conservatives.

Yet, for all of this, having won the presidency, having launched its own special-interest groups, having stuck its foot in the door of the liberal Establishment news media, having huge popular support, the conservative counterrevolution has fallen woefully short of victory. Liberalism still reigns, because it is so thoroughly institutionalized.

Their revolution of the 1940s was successful. We conservatives must now effect a counterrevolution. It is not enough for us to win arguments or to force liberals to admit their past mistakes. The liberal Establishment can afford to let this popular conservative movement express itself, just so long as their own institutions of power and codified statutes and lifetime judgeships are not changed.

Yet that is precisely what must happen. We conservatives must not only win the arguments of the 1980s, we must seize the moment to change the institutions and the laws of the liberal Establishment itself. This will take courage.

PART

II

THE COMPASSIONATE
CONSERVATIVE

CHAPTER

4

In the early 1980s, the political scene gave birth to a new phenomenon—"bleeding heart" conservatives. We are the people who are newly committed to meeting the needs of disadvantaged Americans and believe that the modern conservative movement offers their best hope.

It was the evident failure of the great liberal social programs of the 1960s and 1970s that prompted this phenomenon. Many of us had been conservatives for some time. We were simply emboldened by the growth of our movement and were now anxious to set the record straight that we, too, care about people.

Many others were converted from liberalism. Some, such as Eldrige Cleaver, were former revolutionaries of the 1960s. They had grown disillusioned with their liberal experience. Their conversion had been reluctant and painful. They were quick to let everyone know that they had not abandoned their commitment to the poor or the disadvantaged, but rather felt now that the chain of dependency could only be broken by strong individual initiative.

The compassionate conservatives are now a strong force in the modern conservative movement. They help show the rest of us just how bad the conservative's image is. Even if we are offended by the liberal charges that we don't care about people, that is the public perception, nonetheless. We conservatives are more inclined to talk about the Social Security crisis as if it were a mathematical problem. Liberals, on the other hand, see only the people problem. They talk about the elderly without regard to the cost to the taxpayer.

We conservatives can cry, "Foul," until we are blue in the face. We can point out the hypocrisy of liberals whose budgets and fiscal naiveté brought on the disaster in the first place. We can point out how laughable it is to elect liberals to solve problems that they themselves created. We can criticize the press for running smoke screens to protect liberals by keeping the damaging facts of their failed policy from public view. But all of that means nothing unless we conservatives can convince the blacks, the poor and the elderly that we care about them personally. People are often more concerned that you care about them than that your policy is right.

Compassionate conservatives have also pointed out that the disadvantaged Americans are our true political constituency. If we are going to change America and ensure the rights of the individual and bring about a truly open marketplace, we will need the help of those people who will most benefit by such changes—the disadvantaged.

The failure of the liberal agenda of the 1960s has brought us to a dangerous juncture. The disadvantaged American has few choices. He can no longer choose between this shade of liberal or that and expect things to get any better. With the exception of some important civil rights legislation, liberal policies can be described as well-intentioned failures. If something doesn't change, things will only get worse for America's poor.

As you will see in the next few pages, there are really only two choices left for disadvantaged Americans. They can't stay where they are, embracing the liberal programs that have clearly failed them. One choice is to take a step further to the Left. True, there are still many sidesteps they can take—to socialize medicine, for example, or nationalize the banks or the energy industry. But most of the hope has gone out of such dreams. Britain and France and Sweden have already taken some of those steps and are now trying to crawl back from the brink of disaster.

Some radical voices are calling for an outright Socialist revolution, but there is despair in their voices. The luster is off the worldwide Socialist movement, and they know it. Not only do they have little chance of effecting such a takeover, but even if it came about, it would no longer be what they had once hoped. After the Cambodian, Vietnamese, Russian, Chinese, Ethiopian, Afghan, North Korean, Polish and Hungarian experiences (*ad infinitum*), and to a lesser degree, what has begun to happen in Nicaragua, today's would-be American Socialists no longer really believe in an end to poverty through socialism.

There is another choice. It is the only real hope left to the minorities, the poor and the disabled. And that is a counter-revolution for an open marketplace—a society that would keep a "safety net for the truly needy," while at the same time discovering the risks and rewards of free enterprise.

The liberals will continue to fight such a choice every step of the way. It is as if, having realized the failure and limitations of their own programs, liberals don't even want modern conservative ideas to work. For example, government social workers worry about "job readiness." They warn that even if more jobs were created, most people on welfare haven't the psychological capacity to hold onto them. They suggest that social dependents are like eagles in a zoo, in cages too long. Even if they were set free, they wouldn't know how to fly.

We modern conservatives admit that a return to authentic government-free enterprise would be an adventure, even scary, for those young people who now come from a third generation of welfare families. But to suggest that these "young eagles" cannot fly, that they are bound forever by the environment in which they were born, is bigoted. The liberals were wrong when they first promised that the huge welfare apparatus would only be temporary—a twenty-year program, at best. Why should we believe them now that they say it must be permanent?

THE WELFARE MESS

For the first 150 years after the American Constitution, there was not much of a debate about a welfare system. For one thing, our founding fathers would not have condoned such a function of government as constitutional. For most of American history, it was not even a consideration.

For another thing, a type of socialism, though it was not labeled as such, had already been tried on the North American continent, even before the Declaration of Independence was signed. The Pilgrims at Plymouth were locked into an arrangement that included collective farming and prohibited private ownership of land and property. It was part of their contract. They floundered for two years, and even before their contract expired, they quickly abandoned their economic experiment and became some of America's fiercest free-enterprisers.

The Jamestown experiment was not so lucky. The ideal that stated, "Everyone works and everyone shares," was never realized. While those English adventurers were quite willing to share, very few were willing to put in a good day's work. The colony deteriorated. Most of the food was stolen from the Indians. Nine hundred of the original eleven hundred adventurers died the first year. So John Smith had to resort to the same methods that modern Socialist states often opt for. He declared martial law. Socialism gave way to a benevolent totalitarianism. At the point of a musket, Jamestown colonists were forced to work and share whether they wanted to or not.

In both cases, in North and South, socialism was rejected. A favorite scripture of the American frontier was, "He who does not work does not eat."

American attitudes toward welfare sprang from the Poor Laws of Elizabethan England. The philosophy behind these laws was that charity must be carefully meted out, lest it do more harm than good. It should never replace personal initiative and create total dependency. In every case, there was to be accountability. Most important of all, welfare was meant to be temporary. The individual should be restored as a full member of a productive society.

It is remarkable, but nonetheless true, that this philosophy remained unchallenged for most of American history. Even in the 1930s, when Franklin Roosevelt enacted emergency social legislation to help the country out of a depression, these assumptions were not debated by the two major parties.

The Democrat argument was that such legislation was necessary, but only temporary, to get the country back on its feet. Indeed, some of the programs did run their course and were eventually dropped.

Conservatives of that time argued that such programs might temporarily and artificially relieve an economic crisis but risked compromising the philosophy of individual initiative and free enterprise that had made America great. They warned that it was a drift toward socialism.

THE NEW APPROACH

In the early 1960s, America's philosophy of individual initiative and free enterprise remained unchallenged. The question then became how to deal with the apparent permanence of a welfare state. With each passing year, millions of Americans were caught in the welfare trap, and few, if any, could crawl out. There was growing resentment at the inequities in the welfare system. Some workers complained that "going on welfare paid more." Unwed mothers in poor neighborhoods claimed they couldn't afford to get married and lose the government subsidies that they depended on to take care of their children.

The Kennedy Democrats of the 1960s came up with what appeared to be the best solution of all. They admitted that the welfare system was getting out of hand. They proposed, not an increase in welfare payments, but a change in tactics. The government's objective would be to lift people out of the welfare trap by massive job training programs and by ending minority discrimination.

Charles Murray, in his *Safety Nets and the Truly Needy,* says that the "essence of the unifying appeal was expressed in the slogan, 'Give a hand, not a handout.' It tapped one of the most deeply shared understandings of how the American system was supposed to work." The political appeal was irresistible.[1]

The *New York Times* endorsed Kennedy's program with this editorial: "President Kennedy's welfare message to Congress yesterday stems from a recognition that no lasting solution to the problem can be bought with a welfare check. The initial cost will actually be higher than the mere continuation of handouts. The dividends will come in the restoration of individual dignity and in the long term reduction of the need for government help."[2]

So these new programs would cost a little bit more, they said, but if all those people on welfare had a chance to work, the tax bill would pay for everything.

The young American president was unable to get his program through Congress. Then came his tragic assassination and the great Democratic election victory of 1964. American liberals finally had their chance to legislate every program in their bag. They had an American public still mourning a slain John F. Kennedy and thus sympathetic to his partisan successor. And they had, in President Lyndon Johnson, a master politician.

At that time, it was extremely unpopular to speak about fiscal restraint, and in a post-McCarthy backlash, even to speak of creeping socialism was to commit political suicide. It was time for the centralized government to feed the hungry and to educate the baby boom. There was nothing that the American government could not do. The budget soared, and is still soaring as, twenty years later, some payment must be made toward the interest on the borrowing of the 1960s.

It is difficult for the average citizen to understand mammoth federal budgets. Here is a staggering fact: the fastest-growing segment of the federal budget is the huge portion that goes to pay interest on our debt. In fiscal year 1986, the federal government will spend more for interest payments than on welfare programs! We must, in fact, borrow to pay the interest on the money the government has borrowed. Each year the problem of mounting interest payments increases.

THE RAVAGES OF INFLATION

How could we have gotten into such a position? Couldn't anyone have seen the mathematics? The answer to that question is yes. But few had the courage to stand up to the political rhetoric of the 1960s. "Cost, cost, cost," a liberal politician of the 1960s would say. "All you do is point out how much it costs. But I ask you, can you put a price tag on the value of helping the needy?" Now, how were you supposed to answer that question and still get elected?

The bookkeepers of the 1960s had to have a rationale for this fiscal high-wire act. And so Keynesian economic theory became popularized, just when the liberals needed it most. When the modern conservative movement began to emerge, warning that the whole system was corrupt and would backfire miserably on the very people it was supposed to help, the liberals could answer with some numbers of their own.

John Maynard Keynes argued that private enterprise and competition alone were not enough to bring about full employment and economic recovery. Keynes rejected the philosophy of governmental noninterference in the marketplace, suggesting instead that government needed "purposeful deficit spending to stimulate economic activity."[3]

Assured that the economy would hold up, the Senate and House of Representatives kept spending money, all in the name of the poor. Conservative critics who asked obvious questions were sneered at. The liberals pretended that they were operating on a different intellectual level.

Keynesian economic theory was difficult to understand, but those few who claimed to understand it assured us everything was okay. It would have been appropriate in the 1960s to have reminted our coins, "In Keynes we trust," because his theory was the basis for our economic planning.

For a whole decade, the general population was dazzled with intellectual double-talk. We were placing the wealth of our grandchildren and great-grandchildren in the hands of a few college professors posing as financial experts. We were all hoping that they would be much more successful with the taxpayers' money than they were with their own.

I am tempted to sympathize with the liberal politician of the 1960s. Can we blame him? He was surely well intentioned, wasn't he? He had no idea where this would all lead. He was only duped by trusting the economic technicians or specialists of his day. At least he cared about people.

Yet, many of these "caring" liberal congressmen and presidents were very conservative indeed when it came to their own fortunes. They were quite willing to embrace Keynesian fearlessness and ride right into the face of deficit spending—as long as they weren't risking their own future. Those politicians of the sixties, a few of whom had amassed fortunes, left their money in very safe trust funds, in bond portfolios, and, above all, in land.

Meanwhile, from 1967 to 1983, inflation would reduce the value of the dollars they handed out to disadvantaged Americans from $1.00 to $.337.[4] Yet, when those few conservative senators and congressmen refused to support liberal legislation, they were accused of being "heartless," of "not caring about the poor."

Though the failure of the liberal welfare program was beginning to be evident in the mid-1960s, it became unavoidably clear with the inflation of the late 1970s. Inflation is sometimes defined as too many dollars chasing too few products. When the government needed more cash to pay for its liberal programs, it simply began printing more money. Now, everyone had more dollars, but there was still the same number of goods. The bidding started, and the price of those goods rose.

Inflation became the poor man's tax. He was promised increased subsidies, and then he was paid them in inflated dollars that had become worth less than the promised increases. In one year of the Carter-Mondale administration, inflation reached 13.5 percent. This meant, for example, that the purchasing power of every Social Security check in America was reduced by that same 13.5 percent.

This may not have been what the liberals intended, but it is indeed what happened. The conventional wisdom was that higher inflation would reduce unemployment. Many Republicans as well as Democrats had accepted this notion. In his book, *The American Renaissance,* Jack Kemp traces the concept to the "Phillips curve," named after a British economist. "Insofar as it ever worked, the Phillips curve was based on the unwholesome idea of deceiving workers into taking a hidden cut in real income. Prices would supposedly rise faster than wages, cutting real wages, boosting profit margins, and making it profitable to hire more workers."[5]

It was a nice arrangement. The Democrats could pay off their past debts with cheap inflated dollars. The value of their "entitlements" to the poor could be effectively reduced while the dollar amount held steady or increased. Workers and unions could not complain. They were getting raises, even though they must have scratched their heads and wondered why they were worse off.

THE SOCIAL FAILURE

There are statistics showing that net poverty did decrease during the 1970s, the years in which Lyndon Johnson's war on poverty should have had its effect. Some liberals took great comfort from these facts.

What began to disillusion other liberals was that the decline of the 1970s was no greater than the decline of the decade before it, or even the decade before that. The staggering fact was that, while the number of citizens living below the poverty line dropped by almost one percent a year during the Eisenhower administration, the drop during the Johnson-Nixon-Carter administrations was similar, or even less. But there was a remarkable difference. With the liberal Democrat war on poverty, the United States government was paying sixty-seven times as much to effect the same result!

Some liberals rationalized that they were now dealing with the hard-core poor. The theory was that it took more money to subsidize them. But originally the idea had been to convert them to productive citizenship, not to subsidize them. The *New York Times* had referred to the "initial cost" of such programs, but predicted it would all bring "dividends" later.

John F. Kennedy had announced, "The goals of our public welfare program must be positive and constructive. It must stress the integrity and preservation of the family unit. It must contribute to the attack on dependency, juvenile delinquency, family breakdown, illegitimacy, ill health, and disability. It must reduce the incidence of these problems, prevent their occurrence and reoccurrence, and strengthen and protect the vulnerable in a highly competitive world."[6]

Only ten years later, the overwhelming evidence was in. What followed the enactment of all these programs under Lyndon Johnson was an increase in crime, an increase in divorce and the breakdown of the family unit. With disability insurance and Medicare, there were increases in sickness. Even though there were then two abortions per illegitimate birth, there were increases in illegitimacy. Eighty-five percent of these illegitimate births happened to the poorest 10 percent of Americans, and, predictably, without incentives to become wage earners, there were increases in the welfare population as a whole.

Yes, a larger portion of American citizens were no longer below the poverty line. But remember, that was not the goal. The goal had been to return welfare recipients to the work force by training them. At the time, no one was saying that the whole American experiment was wrong or flawed. Rather they were saying that through discrimination and past inequities, some were disenfranchised or disadvantaged by that system. Government was supposed to pay their way back in, stand them on their feet and then withdraw. Of course, there were the truly needy, also. The idea was to take care of them without defeating their ego or spirit—to help one-parent homes, for instance, without making it "pay" to be a single mother.

The real test of the war on poverty was not how many people were above the poverty level but rather how many were above the poverty level without government subsidy. Was the welfare system doing what it was created to do? Was it converting nonproductive members of American society into productive members?

The answer was absolutely clear—no. The policy had failed. Because a variety of federal programs failed to achieve their lofty ideals and offered a handout instead of a helping hand, many United States citizens came to the conclusion that it "paid to be poor."[7] They did not, and still do not, seek to become independent of the federal subsidies.

THE LIBERALS FIGHT BACK

What do the liberals have to say about this mess?

The most common and most frightening liberal response to its failed welfare policy has been a change in philosophical commitment. I have been careful to show that until the mid-1960s, Republicans and Democrats, conservatives and liberals, from Franklin Roosevelt to John Kennedy, all agreed that the object of the welfare spending was to return welfare recipients to the productive mainstream of American society.

Rather than admit it has failed to do just that, most modern liberals have simply changed the rules and the goal. If they couldn't change reality to fit what they wanted, they simply changed what they wanted reality to fit. In the late 1960s, liberals began saying that the object was not to retrain the poor, but rather quite simply to subsidize them. Of course, that is what they *were* doing. There was no longer any pretense that it was to be temporary. Overnight, by their new definition, their program had become successful and was to be a permanent system for the redistribution of wealth.

How did this happen? What was the liberal rationale? It was simply this: the federal government now had a "moral responsibility" to subsidize the least wealthy members of its society, because the American system was flawed. It was a corrupt system, they charged. If the big boys—the rich and the corporations that ran the system—wanted to continue to enjoy the benefits of such a "flawed system," they were now on notice that they had a responsibility to the people whom the system shut out. The responsibility was shifted from the individual to the American system. Thus, a growing centralized government had the responsibility to bring about "fairness."

In 1967, the man who would serve as Jimmy Carter's secretary of health and human services, Joseph Califano, then an aide to Lyndon Johnson, made a shocking statement to reporters. He said that the best government studies showed that only one percent of the 7.3 million people on welfare were even capable of being returned to self-sufficiency. The philosophical metamorphosis was complete.

At first, the changes were thought to be only semantic. Politicians are always coming up with new words for the same old thing. But as the philosophy began to filter down through the bureaucracy of the American welfare system, the difference was profound. Welfare was no longer called "welfare," it was now called "entitlements." By declaring the American system "basically flawed," the liberals asserted that recipients of government aid were entitled to it. It was their "right."

For years, liberals had been tinkering with Socialist solutions, imposing them here and there in different pieces of legislation. Now, government subsidies began to creep up the ladder. By 1980, half of all subsidized housing went to families above the poverty line. Half of the school lunches and more than a third of the food stamps were going to people above the line as well.[8] The numbers of nonworking Americans expanded rapidly. Instead of helping lower-income families improve their quality of life, more and more were enticed into the welfare trap of increasing dependence, less self-sufficiency and hopelessness.

Of course, it is the liberal welfare program itself that is undeniably the flawed system. But most of today's political leaders have lacked the courage to show true and long-lasting compassion to restore America's disadvantaged.

For example, one of the ideas the liberal Establishment came up with was rent subsidies for the poor. Good idea, right? Well, here is how it worked out. Federal regulations required issuing two checks—one for welfare "entitlements" and one for the rent subsidies (with, of course, all the attendant administrative costs for duplicate paperwork).

However, when recipients began spending the rent subsidies for things other than rent, building owners simply walked away from their sinking investments, defaulting to the cities on the taxes. Then the cities became the landlords, responsible for the upkeep on property that was millions of dollars in the red. By 1978, for example, New York City owned more than ten thousand such buildings, spending more than $75 million a year to keep them up. And, saddled with the same problem that caused the original owners to default, the city was able to collect only 30 percent of the rents.[9]

When New York City Mayor Ed Koch introduced a test project whereby the government would issue checks requiring the endorsement of both the recipient and the landlord, he was promptly denounced by a prominent liberal leader who charged, "Mayor Koch's proposal to force two-party rent checks on welfare recipients as a means of guaranteeing a profit to landlords is cynical, irresponsible and another case of violating the rights of the poor and powerless."[10] This was said despite the fact that most cities simply allowed their buildings to deteriorate, leaving these "poor and powerless" in worse straits than before and defeating the whole purpose of the rent subsidies program. Where is the compassion in that?

The vision of the congressional leaders in Washington became limited to the next congressional election. They killed the New York pilot project before it started, one more example of the lack of courage needed to halt expensive and debilitating programs. Some politicians fear to propose changes because there is "profit in poverty." Many of the special-interest groups peddle fear to the elderly, the unemployed and the poor to keep the politicians from addressing the serious problems of the flawed welfare programs of this country. I know of few that are accomplishing the purposes for which they were created. Most of them are facing financial disaster. Yet few politicians have the courage to pursue the only realistic alternative—an open marketplace, a society that would keep a safety net for the truly needy, while at the same time discovering the risks and rewards of free enterprise.

THE BETRAYAL OF THE
AMERICAN BLACK

CHAPTER

5

I was startled into political reality one Sunday when I heard my son's minister speak. "Just because you are black," he declared, "doesn't mean you have to be a Socialist." I twisted in my seat to measure the crowd. The minister, Carlton Pearson, himself a black and one of the nation's finest young preachers, was challenging his congregation. Half of them were also black, and most of the members of his Tulsa church came from the lower economic levels. What was he telling them?

With the possible exception of the American Indians, no people have suffered more under the liberal Democratic welfare system than American blacks. Because of an accident of modern political history, they have been set adrift, isolated from the very philosophy that could best champion their cause. It is the conservatives who hold the most promise for the black community. In the last decade many great black scholars and revolutionaries have come to this same conclusion, and they are always amazed.

The misunderstanding between the modern conservative movement and blacks came in the early 1960s when Barry Goldwater began his run for the presidency. Goldwater's strong posture against communism aroused support from the South. His emphasis on decentralizing government power attracted southern states-righters. Some of these politicians were racists, almost all were Democrats. They saw that the conservative movement could be used for their own ends, and the consequences of that strategy were tragic, both for blacks and for conservatives.

Liberals like to suggest that the conservative movement embraces the culture and the philosophy and, with them, the racism of the Old South. This is not the case, for Goldwater understood the horrors of discrimination and racism. The fact that his philosophy of government would be used for such ends was and is abhorrent to him. Nor can it be said that southerners were the original conservatives. After all, they had voted for Franklin D. Roosevelt and his welfare programs by huge margins.

Southern racism could, more than anything else, trace its roots to the English class system. When I earlier wrote about the Jamestown colony, I omitted an important piece of history. In 1619, those frustrated Englishmen working at the point of a gun found a way out of their miserable Socialist predicament. That year a Dutch slave ship dropped anchor, and the colonists promptly bought slaves. The Socialist experiment of Jamestown briefly continued. Everyone worked and everyone shared, but the working was done by proxy, and the sharing was equal for everyone but the slaves.

So my earlier suggestion that a type of socialism had been rejected in the North and in the South was not entirely correct. It was true that all *free* men had rejected it as a system for themselves. Still, a measure of that Jamestown socialism was borrowed and used in the slave camps. It was a system imposed on the slaves by the family plantation owners. Sometimes it was a benevolent domination: "We will always feed and take care of you,

Old Sam; don't worry, you worked hard for us." Sometimes it was not so benevolent. But even if we could bring back the most wicked master, he would still argue that his operation was best for the slave. His message to the slave was "You could not make it without us. You would not last a week."

It would be an insult to blacks to equate their suffering under such a system with that of workers in a modern Socialist state. But there are similarities. Like his East German, Russian or Polish counterpart, an American black slave of the Old South couldn't live, work or travel where he wanted without papers and authorization. There was a slave infrastructure to report suspicious strangers or rebellious talk, similar to the block monitors in modern Cuba. There were censorship and control of information. Blacks weren't allowed to read, which brings to mind the hideous order of the Khmer Rouge in 1975 that all Cambodian people who wore eyeglasses were to be executed. And on the borders of the slave South, there were men with guns and even dogs sniffing up and down the rivers that slaves could swim across and be free if they were willing to risk their lives.

Unfortunately, racism was an instrument of both political parties in the South for generations. But the modern American conservative political movement has nothing to do with racism. Rather than having its roots in the South, the modern conservative movement traces its resentment of centralized authority— and thus its appeal to states-righters—to the Pilgrims in the North. The Pilgrims had resented the authority of the king and even greatly feared a national army.

It is this emphasis, more than any other, that makes the modern American conservative movement difficult to understand for those influenced by European thinking. They believe that politics ranges from Left to Right, and that the further to the Right you go, the closer you get to fascism. American conservatives don't fit this pattern. We could hardly fall into the trap of endorsing a dictatorship. Our instincts rebel against it, whether the tyrant is King George or a centralized bureaucracy.

For example, we strongly support local police forces instead of a national police force. It is our fear that federal government subsidies to local programs—whether educational or social—will lead to federal control. It was this commitment to the power and autonomy of local communities that some southern Democratic states-righters exploited in the 1960s.

Yes, it is true some southerners were attracted for the wrong reasons. Yes, it is true the modern conservative movement is still strong in the South. But it is also true that some conservative converts have recognized the error of the old political philosophy and eventually dropped their racism to help pave the way for the new South.

Those who suffered the most in this development of southern political history have been the blacks. For more than a hundred years, they existed with no legal rights at all. Then for almost seventy-five years, they became a one-party people. The blacks were Republicans—it was the party of Lincoln, and that was that. But a vote that Republicans took for granted didn't get very much attention. During the fifty years since Franklin Delano Roosevelt's presidency, blacks have been in the same position, but with another political party. They now get little but rhetoric from their Democratic allies because the bosses are sure of their sentimental attachment, and know that the worst that the blacks can do is sit out an election.

The great irony is that, like the Republican before him, the liberal Democrat sought to do good for the black community. Many of the liberal programs and subsidies were intended to redress past grievances against blacks. But the good intentions have backfired miserably.

As early as 1965, in his controversial Department of Labor report, Daniel Patrick Moynihan warned that "the evidence—not final but powerfully persuasive—is that the Negro family in the urban ghettoes is crumbling." The horrors that liberal Democrat Moynihan saw in 1965 were only the beginning of the terrible consequences of liberal policy. Kennedy had warned that his "welfare program must be positive and constructive. It must stress the integrity and preservation of the family unit." Moynihan had panicked because "twenty-six percent of non-white newborns were illegitimate."

Today, though blacks constitute only 11 percent of the population, 55 percent of all illegitimate births are black. The divorce rate among blacks is twice that of whites. Unemployment runs three times as high. Blacks are the chief target of violent crime. Thirty-four percent of all murders are committed against blacks.[1]

But some liberals resent a discussion of such statistics, and they label as racist anyone who calls attention to the figures. They have a very good reason to be so defensive. For in no way do conservatives suggest that blacks are to blame. No, these statistics are terrible indictments of failed liberal policies.

The blacks have been betrayed. They do not even get the help they have been told they are getting. A black baby born today will, by law, be forced over a lifetime to pay into Social Security roughly sixty thousand dollars, and probably more, because of the poor financial condition of the program. But, according to actuarial tables, he will have a life expectancy of sixty-four years—and thus will die before he ever gets a penny of return from this forced tax.[2] So blacks are subsidizing whites' retirement. How does this demonstrate the self-proclaimed liberal compassion and respect for the dignity of the black community? Even more hypocritical were the ubiquitous liberal promises of more and more increases in government programs, while all along they knew that payment would be made in inflated dollars worth less than the promised increases.

Implicit in every liberal program is the devastating attitude borrowed from the slavemasters of the Old South. "You cannot make it without us. You would not last a week." It is a lie.

THE BLACK CONSERVATIVE
MOVEMENT

There is mounting evidence that while the majority of black leaders have career commitments to the liberal movement, the rank and file are beginning to stir. There are some definite conservative instincts among the black general public, just as there were among organized labor in the late 1960s.

Consider the following data from the National Opinion Research Center. Seventy-three percent of blacks polled wanted increased law enforcement. Ninety-six percent wanted greater classroom discipline. The vast majority were afraid to walk in their own neighborhoods. A surprising 60 percent opposed abortion on demand. Fifty-five percent did not favor increases in welfare, and 85 percent supported the free-enterprise system. Fully 90 percent wanted a constitutional amendment to balance the budget.[3] A good case could be made that the general conservative trend in America is color-blind. Political attitudes among blacks are quite similar to political attitudes among whites.

What proposals do black conservatives have for their people? What do they have to offer? "A lot," says black economist Thomas Sowell, who believes that the new battle cry is economic equality for blacks. Arthur Fletcher, a black Republican and former assistant secretary in the Labor Department, echoes that sentiment. "Blacks now want a piece of the economic pie. There is no social equality unless there is economic equality, and it doesn't make sense to stand on the sideline and pout and puff."[4]

Sowell suggests that the most dramatic economic changes for his people would come with a surprising and simple policy—a reduced minimum wage. Sowell points out that while some American liberals are well intentioned in seeking a higher hourly wage, the result has been devastating for untrained young blacks. As laws mandating higher minimum wages have been passed, black youth unemployment has risen from 25.3 percent in 1966 to 47.3 percent in the 1980s.[5]

Conservatives are so sure that a reduced minimum wage would give jobs to millions of untrained, nonunion black workers that they have even tried to get a summer experimental program through the Congress. This would give the country one summer to see if the conservative theorists are right. And with black youth unemployment so staggeringly high, it would certainly be worth the try.

Not so, says the liberal Establishment. Out of one corner of its mouth, it tells blacks that they don't have to settle for lower wages. Meanwhile, almost half of black youth get no wages at all. Out of the other corner of its mouth, it tells white union workers not to worry. Their jobs are protected. Frustrated conservatives point out that this is the very rationalization used in South Africa to keep blacks out of the white work force, but the irony is conveniently ignored. Carlton Pearson points out this cruel discriminatory cycle: "You can't get work without a union card, and you can't get a union card if you have no work experience."

Another possible answer to the problems of black economic inequality is enterprise zones. By lowering the tax rates and, in some cases, eliminating them altogether, inner-city ghettos could be transformed. Restaurants, shops, businesses and factories would pour in, and with them, thousands of jobs.

At first, liberals were dubious and warned that the value of land would increase. Renters would be forced out. One of their studies worried that life in the inner cities would be "disrupted."

Conservatives did their homework, however, on this issue. Our think tanks show convincingly that jobs would multiply at a much faster rate than prices. A few city governments have made the concept work, reviving their inner cities. Northern Ireland tried a similar approach with great success. Conservatives are offended at the sanctimonious way that liberals refer to "disruption of life" in the ghettos, as if crime-ridden and firetrap tenement houses were historic landmarks in need of preservation in their present state.

Yet the enterprise zones, whose creation would preclude no other program nor deny money that could be spent in other areas, have been consistently tabled with clever parliamentary moves by a liberal Congress. Why? Why won't liberal Democrats allow blacks the chance to see whether a conservative plan would work? There are no risks. No other programs are threatened—not even the welfare programs. If conservatives are right, it would mean millions of jobs for unemployed blacks, and billions of dollars earned, not given. Yet the liberal black leaders will not endorse the proposal. Why not?

Could this be the reason? The black leaders are Democrats. Their careers are at stake. They could not allow Republican solutions. The lifetime curse of the black people is the one-party system.

When the controversial New York mayor Ed Koch took office, he discovered that of the $4.6 million annually allocated for the model cities scholarship program, $2.5 million—over 40 percent of the total monies—were being used for overhead expenses! Furthermore, he learned that most of the administrative personnel in the program had been hired from one powerful Harlem political group. When the staff was slashed back to more reasonable numbers, money was available to grant five thousand scholarships instead of the two thousand formerly given. Koch acerbically observed, "If we had given to the poor all of the money that we have appropriated for the poor over the last twenty years, the poor would be rich."[6]

RESTORING PRIDE

With the concept of enterprise zones stalled, conservatives began looking for something that would have immediate and direct impact on the black community—something that would make a social as well as an economic contribution. They believed they had found it in a proposal to double the one-thousand-dollar-per-person income tax exemption.

Studies have showed that federal, state and local antipoverty programs have spent an astonishing seventy thousand dollars a year for each poor family in America.[7] By simply doubling the per-person income tax exemption, conservatives hoped to wipe out the income tax for poor black families, leaving cash in the hands of the people instead of taking 70 percent of it for the government bureaucracy.

There was a second, more compassionate, purpose behind the strategy. Conservatives saw the double exemption as a way of restoring dignity to the black family unit.

There was a tragic reason why the black divorce rate had reached twice that of whites, and why 55 percent of the nation's illegitimate births were to black mothers. Quite simply, it was the fault of the well-intended but often distorted federal program called Aid to Families with Dependent Children. This program literally induced fathers of poor families to leave home. If the head of a household with children would simply disappear, the federal government would provide his wife with monthly checks, based on the number of those dependent children. In other instances, the program had the effect of encouraging young girls to get pregnant out of wedlock so that they could secure public housing and AFDC payments.

Within one generation, the black family unit, which had survived slavery and ugly racial discrimination, was nearly decimated. Many black fathers, who wanted to be strong role models for their children and wanted to spend their lives with the women they loved, were at a loss. The government had shut them out of most small business enterprises with excessive regulations and licensing procedures that favored already established businesses. White labor unions, with powerful Washington lobbies and hypocritical protection by liberal politicians, shut them out. With the rising minimum wage, even menial jobs began disappearing. For many, welfare was the only real alternative, and it was a trap. Regulations required that savings must be spent. It was difficult, if not impossible, to gather the capital to launch any kind of enterprise to break free of government dependency.

For many, the greatest economic reward and the best security lay in abandoning the home altogether. The more children in the family, the better for everybody concerned if the father would just leave. In its own cruel and impersonal way, the liberal bureaucracy took measures to punish cheaters. Divorces had to be authentic, and a social worker had better not find the father "hanging around."

Conservatives had great hope that the double exemption would pass. But when the proposal reached a liberal Congress, a storm ensued. Would the exemption go to rich families, too? The answer was yes. It would not discriminate.

The argument got bogged down over the fact that the prosperous might benefit as well as the poor. John Kennedy once said, "A rising tide raises all ships," meaning that a prosperous economy and high productivity help everybody. Modern liberals, however, operating on the thesis that the American system is basically flawed, borrowed from Socialist theories. They contended that it is not possible to give to one part of society without taking from another. If conservatives really wanted to help poor families, the liberals would let them, but only at the expense of someone else.

A few conservative black scholars who knew what was at stake argued that the double exemption could be the single most important policy for blacks since the civil rights legislation of the 1960s. They pointed out that a black household with three children would have a tax exemption of ten thousand dollars just to begin with. The process of restoring the black home would begin. Black men would be induced back into the work force. The cost of government welfare would decrease.

Other conservatives, meanwhile, sensing that a little compromise could enable their theories to work, were scrambling for a fallback position. One proposal called for the wholesale transformation of Aid to Families with Dependent Children. It would be replaced with a simple child allowance for families on a limited income, available whether or not the father left home. Other compromises called for allowing the double exemption only for families at the poverty level or below.

In the end, a liberal Congress rejected all of them. It apparently had no courage to try conservative theories that might be successful. Having lost faith in their own programs, liberals had no faith in anybody else's either. In quiet tones, lest they be overheard, liberal congressmen, who for thirty years had voted billions of dollars for welfare programs, told their conservative colleagues that the problems of blacks would have to wait.

THE AMERICAN INDIAN

The status of American Indians is even worse than that of blacks. It is not just welfare that has disabled them, but, quite tragically, it has been oppressive arrangements in the treaties with the United States Congress. I was misquoted frequently during my tenure as secretary of the interior. But one quote that prompted controversy was absolutely accurate. I said, "You don't need to go to Russia to see the failures of socialism. Just go to an American Indian reservation."

The sad truth of that statement has never been challenged. That I dared to tell the truth was what upset the liberals. The media tried to portray the statement as being insensitive to the Indian community. It was, in fact, elected Indian tribal leaders who first expressed this tragic truth to me, as they escorted me through Indian country (their reservations).

The United States government, by law, considers the reservation Indian to be "an incompetent ward." It refuses to allow the individual Indian to make many of the decisions that he should be free to make for his own well-being. As a result, every social problem in America is experienced on the reservation in exaggerated proportions. Unemployment runs 60 percent to 90 percent. Housing problems are huge. Health problems far exceed those experienced elsewhere in the nation, and the education provided in government schools is the poorest anywhere.

Five generations of federal paternalism have sapped the initiative of many Indians. Many tribal leaders do everything in their power to lure their better-educated youth back home in an effort to liberate reservation Indians from the poverty of mind and body dished out by liberal government programs that insult the Indians' intelligence and strip them of self-esteem.

As secretary of the interior, I tried, without success, to get Congress to address these problems. I was resisted time and again. The indifference and lack of "fairness" of the liberal leadership of Congress is demonstrated by their failure for more than eight years to appoint the traditional Committee on Indian Affairs.

The news media elite, meanwhile, had been too preoccupied with their desire to get rid of me. Since they considered me a true conservative in the Reagan cabinet, they followed me everywhere I went, recording dozens and dozens of hours of my speeches, sometimes as many as ten speeches a week. As it happened with other issues, so it was with this one—no matter what I said or how I said it, not one line of my concern or compassion or alarm about what has been happening to the American Indian was ever presented to the American public. The media were not reporting on issues or substance. They were, by their own admission, looking instead for a gaffe, recording thousands and thousands of words in search of a few that could be used against me. Compassion, truth or fairness were not of interest to the liberal members of Congress or the media when it came to the first Americans. What was of interest were their efforts to embarrass me for daring to state the truth.

True compassion for the Indian or black now demands an economic system that provides incentives and an open marketplace. Self-worth, morality and dignity must be reclaimed. The private sector, with its capital, must be brought into the process. The individual must be liberated from the paternalistic control of government.

THE RIGHTS OF
THE VICTIM

CHAPTER

6

In March of 1981, as I was working at my desk at the Department of the Interior, one of my aides rushed in saying the president had just been shot. Things came to a complete halt. What does one do at such a moment? The new president's life and the leadership he represented lay in the hands of the medical team at George Washington University Hospital. Should I go? But what could I do there?

The radio and television broadcasts were indicating that some cabinet officers had gone to the hospital, and my staff members started urging to me to do so as well. "You've got to go," they said. "It's matter of perception. Several cabinet officers are there, showing their concern for the president's health. If you don't go, it will look as if you don't care."

My concern for the president's life was greater than my concern for appearance. I did not go.

To our great relief, we soon heard that the president was out of surgery and alive. About 5:00 P.M., after I had finished most of the work I could do that day, I learned that several cabinet officers and other high administration officials had been meeting continuously in the Situation Room at the White House. Although I realized full well there was nothing I could contribute, I thought at least I should see history in the making.

I entered the White House and was ushered into the wood-paneled, windowless basement room where national emergencies are coped with. Dick Allen, the director of the National Security Council, was there, along with Secretary of Defense Caspar Weinberger, Secretary of State Alexander Haig, Secretary of the Treasury Donald Regan, Secretary of Agriculture John Block, White House Chief of Staff Jim Baker, Counselor to the President Ed Meese, and a dozen or so other White House staffers.

It was controlled confusion. A small television was blaring a continuous stream of reports about the president's condition, with endless replays of the shooting. People kept coming and going, reporting what they had learned from phone calls to the hospital, to the military and to those who knew the location of Vice-President Bush, who was returning from Texas on Air Force Two and would be landing shortly. Ed Meese was to meet him and bring him back to the Situation Room so that the cabinet officers could brief him. At the time, there was a debate about whether the vice-president should land his helicopter on the White House lawn, or be taken to his own quarters, then brought by car to the White House.

In the end, the vice-president made his decision himself. He determined while still in flight that only the president of the United States should land on the White House grounds. He was being careful not to assume any prerogatives of the office, nor did he want even to appear to usurp any powers.

I was studying the behavior of all those in the Situation Room. There were some fascinating exchanges and reactions to a tense and pressure-packed situation that could affect the whole geopolitical picture of the world. Most behaved with distinction. I eagerly awaited the vice-president's arrival, wanting to measure him as well.

I had seriously questioned President Reagan's selection for vice-president, but, because he had made that choice, I had always treated Bush with proper respect, though with little warmth. When the vice-president entered the room, he took firm command, never assuming for himself any inappropriate authority, while showing proper respect for the position into which he might soon be thrust. It was a class performance. He won my total support, and, in the months ahead, my friendship as well.

After Vice-President Bush was given the general briefings, he turned to the roomful of people and asked all those who didn't have a certain security clearance—here he used some initials and numbers—to leave the room. I thought it was perfectly fitting that the former director of the Central Intelligence Agency should issue that order. But nobody moved.

A few moments passed. Jim Baker said, "Those of you who don't have this clearance, please leave the room." No one moved.

Finally, this time with harshness and irritation in his voice, Jim Baker repeated himself. Still no one moved. So I stood up from my position in the corner, behind the vice-president, and said, "I don't even know what those numbers mean. I've never even heard of that classification. I guess I don't have it, so I'm leaving."

The vice-president turned around and said, "Oh, sit down, Jim. Of course you do. You have the highest possible clearance."

When Jim Baker shouted out the name of one of the staff members and ordered her out, most of the others got up and began to file out. They, too, had wanted to watch history in the making.

Caspar Weinberger began the global briefings about the readiness of our forces, and whether any signals had been picked up that the Soviets were trying to exploit the situation.

As one briefing led into another, I was struck by the fragility of our society. One lone gunman with his own anguished personal agenda had thrown our government into turmoil. The assassination attempt was not only threatening the life of a great American president, a man I admired and loved, it was also altering all the priorities of our government. Fleets of ships were moved, troops were alerted, special presidential projects were put on hold. Hundreds of decisions affecting thousands of people costing millions of dollars were caused by one lone criminal act.

Like a lot of Americans, my mind drifted to the Kennedy family, and then to the attempts on the life of George Wallace, and later, President Ford. I wondered about the press coverage. Like all the other would-be assassins, the young man would be guaranteed his spot on the covers of our national magazines. Even as the evening wore on, the television networks were carefully sifting through his biography and passing it along. The whole process seemed important to the media. America is always hungry for information at such times, yet the detailed coverage almost appears to celebrate violence and contribute to its recurrence.

As we were being briefed on the president's condition and the world scene, we were also told about our friend Jim Brady, the president's press secretary, who had been shot in the head. What a tragedy! Would he make it? Every report was grim. As I listened to the details of the senseless attack, I thought about all of the other innocent victims of violence in America. About the woman who is raped and then, throughout the judicial process, becomes a victim again and again. Or the strong young man whose youth and fearlessness are no guarantee of his safety. He can be cut down as randomly as anyone else.

It was now dark outside. Out on the streets of our nation's capital, beyond the secure walls of the White House with its layers and layers of security devices, video cameras, fences and armed guards, ordinary citizens walked in fear. How defenseless the individual victims of crime must feel! There was no nation praying for them. There was no guarantee that the police would be efficient, or the courts just. It struck me how very alone the victims are.

Never in my wildest imagination did I think, as the networks endlessly reran the videotape of the shooting of the president, that the young gunman would someday be declared not guilty. The whole story seems a symbolic caricature of how helpless our society is and how twisted our sense of justice has become. If the president's attempted assassin, whose act was seen by the world, is not guilty, then who is? If the president of the United States, with his legions of secret servicemen, is not safe, then who is?

CRIME IN AMERICA

In 1985, nearly 25 million American households will be victimized by crime. A forcible rape in Reno. A criminal homicide in Houston. A malicious arson in Minneapolis.

These are the cases you hear about. They become spectacular news. But in the time it takes to read this paragraph, hundreds of other crimes will take place. And they, too, will become statistics in the Crime Index of the Department of Justice. There will be aggravated assault, auto theft, larceny, burglary, prostitution, vandalism, embezzlement, counterfeiting, sex offenses and so much more. The list seems endless.

An all-time high in criminal activity was reached in 1980. What happened was tragic. A murder every twenty-three minutes. A rape every six. A robbery every fifty-eight seconds, a burglary every eight seconds.[1] We conservatives like to point to the 4 percent drop in crime in 1982 and to the 7 percent drop in 1983 as evidence of what a slightly tougher Supreme Court and more aggressive law enforcement can do. But even if liberals were to grant us that point (and I doubt very much that they would), by any measurement, historical or contemporary, the level of crime in this country is intolerable.

THE LIBERAL COURTS

Perhaps no case in recent history has had such an impact on the American criminal justice system as *Miranda v. Arizona.* Ernesto Miranda was found guilty of the kidnapping and violent rape of his victim. Yet, in 1966, by a five-to-four vote, the Supreme Court of the United States set Miranda free. The decision was that arresting police officers had failed to inform him of his constitutional rights.

There was an immediate protest. Conservatives were outraged, citing that police forces were already underpaid, understaffed and overloaded with paper work. Conservatives wondered why policemen should be required to give legal advice to their suspects. Most galling of all was the fact that prior to *Miranda,* there had been no legislation, no election, no referendum or even warning. Police could be taught how to "read the rights" to any future suspect, but in the meantime, thousands of cases would be thrown out of the courts. The rules, indeed the law itself, had been changed. If policemen and prosecutors wanted to salvage any of their cases, they would have to scramble as best they could.

The *Miranda* decision, however, was only the most famous example of a liberal Supreme Court determined to "safeguard the rights of the accused." Having an even greater impact was the so-called exclusionary rule, which prohibited improperly obtained evidence from being used in courts. It sounded fair enough, but the actual application of the rule by liberal judges, appointed during almost a generation of liberal rule, created a bonanza for defendants. Confessed killers walked free because an arresting officer failed to follow proper procedures. One case involved a policeman who had failed to rush across town to obtain a search warrant before searching a garbage can for a discarded weapon.

Lower courts and even parole boards followed the spirit of the times. A famous case involved Barry Braeseke, who was arrested for the murders of his mother, father and grandfather. Yes, he was advised of his right to remain silent and to have an attorney present. But he insisted on speaking, "off the record." Braeseke confessed on three different occasions. He even told his story to millions of viewers on CBS's "60 Minutes." Yet the California Supreme Court, in a four-to-three decision, suppressed Braeseke's confessions and overturned his conviction, on the grounds that he did not know what he was doing when he confessed.

One would imagine that overcrowded prisons might have alerted judges that the new leniency of the sixties and seventies wasn't working. Once more, liberals simply blamed the system. Citing overcrowded jails and penitentiaries, judges rushed into plea bargains with prosecutors, reducing sentences and, in some cases, turning even repeat offenders loose on parole.

This leniency was vividly illustrated in the final report of President Reagan's 1982 Task Force on Victims of Crime. It noted that "a man was convicted in 1974 of sexually assaulting a child. He repeated the offense and, in 1980, was convicted again and sentenced to 18 months. He served seven months. After that conviction, he was arrested again for molesting a seven-year-old. He was released on bail, and, while out on bail, he molested yet another child."[2] Between 1960 and 1970, crime, already at intolerable levels, increased another 60 percent.

Throughout this whole process, liberals kept championing the rights of the accused, not the victims. They spoke of the constitutional right of a swift and fair trial. Of the Fourth Amendment, which promised "the right of the people to be secure in their persons, houses, papers and effects, against unreasonable searches and seizures." And of the Eighth Amendment, which promised that "excessive bail shall not be required nor excessive fines imposed, nor cruel and unusual punishment inflicted."

These amendments were not new. They had, after all, been around for a couple hundred years. It was the liberals' interpretation of these amendments that was new. In their headlong and single-minded effort to guarantee "the rights of the accused," liberals seemed to ignore the rights of citizens to enjoy "life,

liberty, and the pursuit of happiness." The whole judicial system
left the victims of crime helpless. The law did not require that
they be informed of the progress of criminal cases. They had no
legal right to be heard or consulted regarding plea bargains,
restitution or sentencing.

Many people believed that justice had become a mockery. Right
and wrong were no longer based on common sense or on instinc-
tively held values or principles. Liberal justice had become amoral.
The purpose of law had been lost and citizens had become
disillusioned.

Thomas Jefferson once wrote, in a prescient appreciation of
how ambiguous American justice in the wrong hands could be,
"Laws are made for men of ordinary understanding, and should
therefore be construed by the ordinary rules of common sense.
Their meaning is not to be sought for in metaphysical subtleties,
which may make anything mean everything, or nothing, at
pleasure."[3]

CONSERVATIVES STEM THE TIDE

The process of reversing years of the liberal trend in our judicial system has already begun. With the Nixon-Ford-Reagan
Supreme Court appointees, there has developed a "good faith"
exception to the controversial exclusionary rule. Now, if a police
officer is acting on a search warrant that is later determined to
be defective, the evidence he obtains will not necessarily be
thrown out of court. The determining factor will be whether the
officer was acting in good faith. Justices have already begun to
reverse the radical interpretation of the Fourth Amendment.
Police may now inspect an open field for drugs or seize evidence
that is in plain view.

The conservative agenda for criminal justice in this country
is now gaining support. Some state legislatures are already reversing the liberal trend.

Modern conservatives call for courts to impose higher bail or even deny bail for defendants who are deemed likely to commit additional crimes if freed, especially if they have prior criminal records. Violent behavior requires a tough response. If a man rapes a woman, denying bail is not necessarily "excessive."

Second, conservatives support laws mandating minimum sentences for crimes of violence, so that even a lenient judge cannot contrive a sentence unequal to the crime. Perhaps the most "head-shaking" statistic in the whole debate about American justice is that the average murderer spends less than six-and-a-half years in prison. Money is evidently more precious than life—or at least more powerful with our liberal judges and parole boards—for, on average, a bank robber will serve twice as much time.

Third, conservatives recommend greatly reducing the power of parole boards to release criminals, unless certain standards are met. The most popular conservative theories include a merit system that awards points for a convict's behavior and his or her response to rehabilitation and restitution efforts. Most important, conservatives suggest that the crime victims and relatives be included in the parole process.

Fourth, for their own sake as well as for that of their victims, convicted criminals should be required to repay the victims of their crimes with personal assets or dollars earned in the prison system or even after release. No person who has committed a violent crime should be shielded from the great suffering and pain he or she has caused the living and wounded left behind. Swindlers, extortionists and thieves should not be allowed to serve six months in a prison and then walk away from the responsibility of having defrauded another human being of his or her private property. In addition to paying fines to the state, such convicted criminals should have their wages taxed until they have repaid every penny they have stolen.

Fifth, victims and relatives should have copies of court transcripts if requested.

Sixth, victims should be consulted by prosecutors and judges during plea bargaining.

Seventh, victims should be heard by judges, and, if necessary, legislation should guarantee them that right. Many jurists now accept input from victims before sentencing, but many others refuse to consider it.

Eighth, the federal government should contract with private and state institutions that have proven success in criminal rehabilitation. One of the great disappointments of the federal effort to reduce crime and bring about rehabilitation is the government's inability or unwillingness to utilize the private and state organizations with high rates of rehabilitation.

Ninth, a new verdict should be established: "guilty, but insane." While courts should have greater flexibility in determining a proper sentence for mentally disturbed criminals, there should be mandatory minimum sentences for crimes nonetheless. "Not guilty by reason of insanity" has become a wide-open door allowing thousands of defendants to escape responsibility for their actions. The National Institute of Mental Health released a study in 1984 that included interviews with ten thousand people. It determined that one in every five adult Americans, or 29 million people, suffer from mental problems."[4] But there must be some minimum degree of accountability, even for the emotionally and mentally disturbed. There is no inducement for disturbed people to discipline their own emotions and urges when a young man can open fire on the president of the United States, put a bullet into the head of the president's press chief while the whole world watches, and then be acquitted.

Tenth, conservatives have called for a discriminate use of the death penalty. There is ample evidence that the probability of death is a deterrent. Nature does not excuse people if they violate its laws. If they fail to practice laws of hygiene or nutrition, they may die of disease. If they are careless, they may die in an automobile accident. People who can't swim may drown if they insist on launching out into water over their heads. Even emotionally disturbed people learn to respect laws of nature, which cannot be compromised.

Our opponents ask how we can be pro-life when it comes to abortion, and pro-death regarding capital punishment. The answer is our link to absolutes and moral values, in this case, the laws of Moses, and our reverence for human life. Conservatives see the term *capital punishment* as a misnomer. Most of us would agree with liberals in saying that it serves no purpose as punishment. But conservatives do see it as a legitimate deterrent.

As attorney Frank Carrington, executive director of the Victims' Assistance Legal Association, says, "Liberals almost invariably raise the sanctity of human life when advancing their arguments for the abolition of the death penalty. The life to be sanctified is, of course, always that of the murderer, never that of the victim."[5]

IS AN UNFAIR SYSTEM TO BLAME?

Liberals accuse conservatives of taking a superficial approach to criminal justice. They say we are more concerned with punishing criminals and policing the country than we are with studying antisocial behavior and eliminating the causes of crime.

According to liberal dogma, society itself is to blame. At one point, liberals toyed with the idea that antisocial behavior was related to poverty. Charles Silberman advanced this idea in his book, *Criminal Violence, Criminal Justice,* adding the liberal thesis that "if we are to reduce crime, we will have to recognize that more punishment is not the answer."[6]

Studies from liberals' own think tanks soon debunked this idea. Criminal demographics defied any economic stereotype. America's newest young criminals come from middle class or even wealthy homes as well as the ghetto.

We conservatives have, from the beginning, challenged the whole idea of a crime-poverty connection. America's crime rate has risen with her wealth. Her crime rate has grown many times higher than that of India, for instance, even though the difference in wealth between our two countries is staggering. Why would a beggar on the streets of Calcutta starve to death rather than steal food to live, even when his punishment would mean only a jail sentence with regular meals? Because being poor does not in itself force him to crime.

A shrewder liberal position, and one that has endured to this day, is that crime breeds among the disenfranchised. It is the people who have been discriminated against, liberals insist, or the people to whom society has been unfair who are more likely to violate the law, if they have to, to "get even."

We conservatives, however, challenge this thesis. We simply don't believe that the rise of crime can be blamed on the American system, which liberals would have us believe is flawed and filled with inequities. After forty years when liberal power has been brought to bear on these alleged causes of crime, with every opportunity for experiments by government agencies, with redistribution of wealth and with liberal federal courts, the crime rate has increased. If fairness were indeed the issue, and a liberal program did indeed redress it, then crime should have been going down, not up. Sometime around the 1930s, and again in the 1960s, crime should have begun to decrease as the champions of liberalism saw their legislation passed and their court appointments confirmed. However, the very opposite occurred.

DOES CRIME PAY?

Conservatives are often asked why we approach the issue of crime from the standpoint of controlling the criminal instead of studying the cause of crime.

The answer is that we conservatives believe we know the cause of crime and its increase, and liberals are upset because we won't buy their explanation. We contend that the violence in our society can be traced to the individual's loss of moral absolutes and departure from the traditional values and principles upon which our nation was founded. The degradation of the value of life and self-esteem makes it easier for people to assault or injure other human beings. Property values have little significance if human values don't count for much. If the government says something is wrong or is a crime and then doesn't believe its own words enough to enforce them, why should anyone else respect the system?

A criminal law professor from Fordham University in New York City told me that, as a practical matter, the stealing of a car in New York is not now a crime. Over a hundred thousand cars are stolen there each year, yet there are only about a dozen persons in New York prisons serving time for car theft. The judicial system—cops and courts—simply does not have sufficient resources to enforce the law. And an unenforced law is no law at all.

For some in New York and elsewhere, crime pays. If a teenager wants to go for a joyride, he simply hot-wires the nearest nice-looking car and goes wherever he wants until the gas tank registers empty. If someone needs a quick dollar, he merely grabs a clean, late-model automobile and sells it to the "right" party. What are the costs to the thief? Virtually nothing. The same is true of mugging, burglary, rape, larceny, arson. The string of unpunished crimes seems endless.

Again the solution is the "marketplace." The costs for improper behavior must be high enough and certain enough that society can maintain order. There must be internal and external costs for each person to consider before he chooses his behavior. Is he willing to pay the price? If he wants to go for a joyride, does he buy a car, rent one or steal it? Most of us would think this a very simple ethical decision to make, but a hundred thousand persons in New York City decided it was "cheaper" to steal than to exercise either of the other two options.

What are the costs? The internal costs to be weighed are the moral considerations, theological values and social standards in a person's mind. External values include dollars, peer pressure, potential for punishment (physical or mental) and actual punishment if caught. If society (family, schools and community) has not implanted moral values and teachings in its members, and if there is no punishment for antisocial activity, it becomes more and more difficult for individuals to determine what is right and wrong. Why not take that good-looking red sports car left sitting at the curb for "my convenience?"

Crimes that were once done in the dark and in secret are now committed in the daylight and with open arrogance. Groups of young boys and girls move through the streets and subways of our communities, gaining confidence from their numbers. Their actions mock a government that has shown more concern for the perpetrators of crime than for the victims.

It is true that prison reforms are needed in the American prison system to improve the living conditions, counseling and education of the criminal. However, the idea of punishment for wrongdoing has faded as the purpose of prisons. With all the recent preoccupation about the criminal's welfare, some citizens and potential victims have realized that their own privacy, emotions, physical safety and property are at risk.

To protect themselves, many who fear they may be the victims of crime have taken it upon themselves to protect their own interests. Assertiveness training, ju jitsu, karate, defense against rape, instruction in how-to-be-robbed-and-live, as well as how to handle shotguns and handguns, are all in vogue today because of the fear that government may not give enough protection.

The year 1985 may be a watershed for public debate about the individual's role in rescuing the attacked from the attacker. In New York City and Chicago, in large towns and small cities, citizens have shot attackers who were threatening to rob subway riders, store owners and other innocent victims. As could be expected, some liberals have charged that citizens should not carry or even own handguns because the result of a shooting could be more severe than the potential crime. Other advocates have championed a citizen's right to defend himself as well as his moral obligation to protect someone else, even if a gun had to be used to stop the attacker. The American people have rallied to the defense of private citizens who have protected both themselves and others; they too feel frustrated with the level of crime in America.

We conservatives are quite willing for the whole debate about crime to continue—with conservatives blaming it on a loss of moral values, and liberals suggesting that the fault lies in the inequities of our flawed system. While we argue, however, crime continues to prey on the most vulnerable members of our society. It is the poor, the elderly, the minorities and the children who must suffer during this liberal-conservative tug-of-war.

Crime is an emergency problem that demands immediate action. We conservatives seek to establish a government that would be as responsive and conscientious in protecting the rights of the victims as it is in faithfully protecting the rights of the accused.

The immediate concern of conservatives is that the criminal be incarcerated in order that society be protected. Liberals may be right when they say that throwing a child abuser in prison is a rather superficial way to handle a profound and complex social problem. But it is not considered superficial by parents of other children who could be abused if the criminal were set free. This may be, as the liberals say, "putting Band-Aids on the problems," but it is much more than a Band-Aid to those innocent members of our society whose lives can be saved by efficient law enforcement and a swift judicial process.

To those who would say that the conservative approach to criminal justice is too simple, I would add two thoughts. Law was meant to be simply understood and enforced. And we need to explore how great the threat is to the potential victims of crime.

A VIOLENT SOCIETY

CHAPTER

7

Modern conservatives see crime as only one manifestation of a society that has grown increasingly violent in the home and hospitals, on the highways and over the airwaves.

The violence on America's highways claims an annual human life toll equal to the entire Vietnam War, the longest in America's history! Yet we have become numb. Journalists give the statistics only token acknowledgment on holidays, like parishioners who attend church only on Christmas and Easter. Everyone ignores the warnings of psychiatrists who point to highway violence as evidence of an angry, depressed and suicidal society. Meanwhile, the killing goes on.

Then there is the great revolution in American art. From our music to our motion pictures, genius and subtlety are being crowded out by shock and violence.

And always, everywhere around us, at the root of much of our suffering is our abuse of alcohol and drugs, which sap the energy and vitality of some of our greatest artists. All the suffering notwithstanding, it has become fashionable for the elitists in our society to enjoy cocaine. For comedians, chemical abuse is something to joke about, even though other comedians have lost their lives because of it. It has spawned an insider's language that rock musicians speak to our children.

Don't think for a moment that you have escaped, even if you are one of the rare American families untouched by drug or alcohol abuse. With the advent of chemical abuse and the growing acceptance of violence in our society, life has been cheapened. Every one of us, from the eldest grandparent to babies in their mothers' wombs, has been devalued.

A QUESTION OF LIFE

The liberal Establishment is fond of polling the American people with the following question: do you favor an amendment to the Constitution to make abortion illegal? For many complicated reasons, a majority will usually say no. But such polls provide a very simplistic way to dismiss what is a very large and growing pro-life movement. The issue is much greater than whether or not abortion should be legal.

Liberals like to say that the whole point is one of "freedom of choice." They are indignant over the idea that someone else could tell a woman what she can or cannot do with her own unborn baby. Yet few women subjected to pro-choice counseling are ever sent to prolife clinics to review the consequences of a decision to terminate a life. The question of whether that baby is indeed a human life is often rejected as irrelevant. Liberals suggest that the question is only a ruse, an excuse for some religious conservatives to impose their will. Implicit in the liberal argument is the idea that offering someone a choice is, in itself, virtuous.

This is nonsense. Citizens are not given the choice whether or not to steal. They are not given the choice whether or not to kill their three-year-old child (though, as frightening as it sounds, sometimes citizens may legally do just that). No, the question is not one of choice, but rather at what point the mother's freedom violates her baby's. When is a baby a person? Some may argue that it is not an easy question to answer. Whether or not it is easy, conservatives argue that we must give the benefit of the doubt to life and stop abortions.

For some of us, abortion is a theological question that raises our moral obligation to the unborn. But there are a great many others involved in the prolife movement who are never identified if a pollster's question is phrased just right. For example, there are many who oppose abortion except in cases of incest or rape. The numbers of these conservative people are usually added to the liberal side of the question when any poll is taken. (A notable exception was a *Newsweek* poll taken by the Gallup organization. When asked if they favored a ban on abortion except in the case of rape, incest, or danger to a mother's life, 58 percent said yes. Only 36 percent said no.)

There are many other conservatives who wish only to see an end to the government subsidy of abortion. They would say, "If it doesn't violate your conscience to abort your baby, that's your business. What offends me is that the government taxes me to pay for something that violates my own conscience and faith." They, too, frequently show up in the polls to be in favor of abortion.

The fact that a group in our society cannot afford abortions should not dictate that taxpayers pay for them. Should the public also be taxed to help finance the pornography industry? Since we have freedom of speech and there are poor people who cannot afford pornography, shouldn't the government make it available?

Of course, that would be ridiculous. Yet this is exactly the rationale liberals are using to demand taxpayer's money to subsidize an abortion industry that is even more controversial than pornography. To many conservatives, it is shameful killing.

Then there are conservatives who are frightened by where the abortion phenomenon has led us. This latter group will eventually become the largest, and will, we hope, someday tip the scales in the whole debate. In 1984, Vice-President George Bush, considered by some to be a moderate on the subject, announced that "fifteen million abortions are enough."[1] By 1985, the practice reached assembly-line proportions, for there were three abortions every minute in this country. As with Bush, the attitude of many has changed.

In 1973, soon after the Supreme Court ruled in favor of abortion on demand, Dr. Everett Koop, now the United States surgeon general, presented a paper warning that the decision would "lead to such cheapening of human life that infanticide would not be far behind." It is this step in the progression, more than anything else, that is sending a chill down the spines of those with any appreciation of recent history, and is causing a great many in the medical and legal professions to reconsider the wisdom of the Supreme Court's decision. At what point does the killing stop? When is a person a person? And when does he or she have rights?

"I don't think abortion is ever wrong," says Virginia Abernethy, a psychiatrist at Vanderbilt University School of Medicine. "As long as an individual is completely dependent upon the mother, it's not a person."[2] Newsweek took up the abortion controversy in a cover story in January 1985. In explaining Abernethy's view, a position that Newsweek said is shared by other pro-choice theorists, the magazine explained, "An individual becomes a person only when he or she becomes a responsible moral agent—around three or four, in Abernethy's judgment. Until then, she thinks, infants, like fetuses, are non-persons. Defective children, such as those with Down's Syndrome, may never become persons. The claim they have on persons, she says, is compassion, not a moral right to life."[3]

In Ideals of Life, Millard Everett suggests that "No child be admitted into society of the living who would be certain to suffer any social handicap—for example, any physical or mental defect that would prevent marriage or would make others tolerate his company only from the sense of mercy."[4]

To the increasing practice of allowing handicapped infants to starve to death in their hospital cribs, Dr. Koop offered this warning: "If indeed we decide that a child with a chronic cardio-pulmonary disease or a short bowel syndrome or various manifestations of brain damage should be permitted to die by lack of feeding, what is to prevent the next step which takes the adult with chronic cardio-pulmonary disease who may be much more of a burden to his family than the child is, or the individual who may not have a short bowel syndrome but who has ulcerative colitis, and in addition to his physical manifestations, has many psychiatric problems as well, or the individual who has brain damage—do we kill all people with neurological deficit after an automobile accident?"[5]

Even more tragic and horrifying is the systematic killing of infants who are expected to develop mental retardation or some other chronic dependency on their parents. In this case, the liberal argues, "Stay out of it. It's between the parent and the doctor. After all, we don't want some conservative moralist imposing his idea of right or wrong on someone else. Whose baby is this, anyway?"

To be sure, infanticide is, with some exceptions, not yet legal outside of the hospital. The newspapers will report, from time to time, shocking and horrible stories of child abuse—sometimes by violent or chemically dependent parents who have locked their children in a closet for several months, or, like their medical counterparts in the highly civilized neonatal hospital nurseries, who have starved an infant to death in its crib. Yet these parents will be hauled before us as freaks, and we will chronicle what they have done with revulsion.

But what is the difference between these child abusers and doctors who, in consultation with parents, will do the same? Why are such cases so fiercely defended by liberal human rights activists? Whose rights are being advanced?

Dr. Koop, in an address to the American Academy of Pediatrics, said, "Because a newborn child has the possibility of any of

these problems in later life, does this give us the right to terminate his life now? If it does, then I suspect that there are people
in this room who have chronic dyspnea, who may have oxygen
dependency at night, who may be incontinent, who may have a
contracture, who may have a sexual handicap, and I trust that
none of you are mentally retarded, but let's carry it to its logical
conclusion. If we are going to kill the newborn with these poten-
tials, why not you who already have them?"[6]

Civilized people should never condone the use of abortion, infanticide or euthanasia to destroy the lives of innocent people
for the benefit of selfish interests, elite ideals, convenience or any
other such purpose. Yet centralized governments of both the Left
and Right have done just that in Russia, Cambodia, Germany,
Iran and other countries. Government leaders have adopted "killing policies" to create "the superior race" or to reduce economic
costs to their society or to make it more convenient for the present
selfish generation. Has America learned nothing from these les-
sons of history?

VIOLENCE IN THE ARTS

If the life of an unborn infant or a small child is censored, there
is little public or media reaction. But to raise the issues of pornography or violence in the arts provokes a quick protest from the
liberal Establishment, particularly from the media. Once again, it
was a liberal Supreme Court decision that opened the floodgate.
Liberals claimed they were defending freedom of speech—but
was there no true freedom before (or without) X-rated movies
and child pornography?

Conservatives argue that we had prospered for two centuries
without such "freedoms." It is imperative for society to apply restraints to itself. While liberals label conservatives as "book burn-
ers," we still contend that liberals themselves routinely practice
ideological censorship. For example, they have successfully blocked
in court the telecasting of antiabortion documentaries. Invoking

the "fairness doctrine," the court adopted the astonishing "logic" that the liberals had not yet produced a documentary of equal impact. The rest of their successful complaint consisted of warnings that the medical and scientific data used in the documentary could be misunderstood by the layman.

Too frequently, liberals, while defending the peddlers of hardcore pornography, have been successful censors, by objecting to the licensing of conservative religious radio and television stations. Liberals oppose the expression or the publication of views and values that challenge their own rigid perspective. Conservatives are concerned that liberals have for the last fifty years been winning this battle over whose ideas can be expressed. Our society is suffering the results.

Some liberals still insist that motion pictures, magazines and television don't make people do things. However, most will grant that advertisers don't pay up to a million dollars a minute for television time if that money doesn't translate into activity. If brief commercials that people only half notice have such impact, how can our society be so sure that people are immune to the hours and hours of violent drama?

There are, for example, the reported cases of at least twenty-five young people who, after viewing *The Deerhunter,* died playing Russian roulette. Months later, a high school honor student chopped his mother, father and sister to death and left a brother a quadriplegic soon after watching a television movie of the Lizzie Borden ax murders. Within two weeks after the movie *The Burning Bed* aired on national television, two wives were set on fire and burned to death by their husbands. A gang of girls in California raped an innocent classmate with a broom handle after seeing the same scene in a violent television movie. But the courts refused to hold the television network accountable.

Today, we don't have to theorize. The facts are in. In May of 1982, the National Institute of Mental Health analyzed surveys and reports involving more than a hundred thousand television viewers in dozens of nations. Their conclusions were overwhelming that "violence on television does lead to aggressive behavior."[7] A typical high school graduate will spend twice as much time watching television as he will in the classroom.[8] According to a *Reader's Digest* article, it amounts to "ten years of forty hour weeks."[9] During high school, he or she will have witnessed twenty-five thousand deaths.

Leonard Eron, a University of Illinois psychology professor, reviewed the television viewing habits of 184 boys at age eight. When they turned eighteen, he checked again and found that the more violent the television viewing had been in early childhood, the greater were the odds of violence and antisocial behavior in the teenage years.[10] A prestigious study by William Belson, a British psychologist, concluded that teenaged viewers of heavy violence were 47 percent more likely to be violent themselves, compared with the norm group.[11] We have raised our own violent generations.

America has been blind to the logical conclusions of the moral debate. The issues weren't only free speech or censorship and the neutrality of ideas. Conservatives believe that when you cheapen or degrade human life in one dimension, it is devalued in every aspect. What more needs to be done to demonstrate that not only are we what we eat, we are what we see and hear?

Some liberals respond that attempts by conservatives to boycott advertisers who support violent or sexually exploitive films and television represent a demagogic, frightening assault on First Amendment rights. Liberals themselves are not hooked on X-rated movies, of course, nor do they want to see child pornography or bodies chopped up or dismembered with electric saws. Rather, they say that these are sacrifices we must all make to protect freedom of the press and speech. But we conservatives simply refuse to accept this argument. We champion parents who responsibly turn off the television and who demand alternative literature assignments for their school-aged children. We applaud youths who resist peer pressure and "the right to do your own thing." The fruits of the permissive interpretation of the Constitution are the degradation of our nation, her character and her morality. Freedom must carry with it social accountability for the dignity and worth of the individual.

THE BEACH BOYS

I got caught up in the whole censorship controversy when reports began coming to my desk about the ever-increasing problem of drugs and violence at the annual July 4 rock festivals on the mall in our nation's capital. Shortly after the 1982 celebration, at which The Grass Roots, a pop and rock band, performed, a mother representing the Washington chapter of Parents for Drug-free Youth complained to me about the use and sale of drugs at that free public concert sponsored by the Department of the Interior. Park police had arrested forty adults for offenses such as assault and disorderly conduct. Many people who were on drugs had annoyed others who had come simply to enjoy the music. Six hundred and sixty-seven people were treated at the first aid station, many for drug-related problems. Some five hundred young people had participated in an advertised "smoke-in," defying the police to arrest them for smoking marijuana.

While there were, no doubt, many thousands of nonabusers among that college-aged crowd, the report of illegal drug use was disturbing. Interior Department park police stated they had reached the point where they could no longer concentrate on drug-related activities and, at the same time, maintain order among the several hundred thousand people gathered for the concert. So they let the drugs and their accompanying violence run their course.

Part of my responsibility as secretary of the interior was to oversee the nation's monuments and the parks and grassy malls of the capital. Since drug use is prohibited in all of the national parks, I decided that, to discourage drug and alcohol use, the next July 4 celebration would be reoriented toward the family, rather than toward youth alone. In November 1982, I issued a memorandum to the National Park Service directing that future July 4 celebrations "point to the glories of America in a patriotic and inspirational way that will attract the family."

Nearly five months later, newspapers and media flashed across America the "news" that I had canceled the Beach Boys concert. I had, in fact, done no such thing. I had not used their name, nor had any reference been made to them either directly or indirectly by me or anyone else. I learned later that they had not even been booked in the first place.

The controversy actually arose because I was a conservative. Members of a liberal press saw an opportunity to create a controversy by censoring the facts and avoiding the real issues. Indeed, their strategy worked surprisingly well. When the *Washington Post* first announced that I had "banned rock music" from the celebration, it only mentioned that the Beach Boys had performed in the past. Yet before we knew what was happening, banner headlines proclaimed that I had banned the Beach Boys. I was astonished. The impression was given that since the Beach Boys had appeared on the July 4 stage two years earlier, there was something sinister about the fact that they were not to perform this particular year.

The White House was also caught in the media's net of half-truths and innuendos. I suppose it was unreasonable to assume that White House officials would focus on drug-abuse issues when the media asked only for comments on music groups. During other flare-ups with the press, the White House had backed me.

I was in the middle of quite a controversy. The original and central issue of violence and drugs flowing freely within the very shadow of the Lincoln and Washington monuments was never even mentioned by the media. In its place was a media-contrived political problem. Liberals and the rock music radio stations were calling for my resignation. It was an absurd, but job threatening, political situation. If knowledge of popular music groups had anything to do with administering the Interior Department, the Senate should have grilled me on the subject during my confirmation hearings! (Did calling for a patriotic and inspirational program prohibit a performance by the Beach Boys? Apparently it did in the minds of my opponents. But I had never suggested that the Beach Boys were unpatriotic.) One would assume that, in all fairness, the professionals in the media would have corrected themselves when the facts did not fit the created story. However, the misrepresentations and censorship continue to date (not only about the July 4 celebration but about other Interior issues as well).

Despite all the controversy, my decision that the July 4 celebration should be family-oriented proved to be sound. During the 1983 Fourth of July observance, there were *no* reported injuries from drug overdoses or broken bottles, and the number of people seeking medical treatment was only one-tenth that of 1982.

Leaders have a duty to champion wholesome community values, regardless of media censorship and distortion. Society must teach and promote values that will sustain a new generation. It is cowardly and irresponsible to bow to violence in the cinema and to the celebration of drugs in music on the premise that fashion and art can never be right or wrong, moral or immoral. To assert that they are above the law and therefore free of responsibility for their influence is injurious to a nation—as America has proved to herself.

ALCOHOL AND DRUG ABUSE

Throughout the long years of the Vietnam War, the television network news carefully tabulated the mounting death toll. It was a sickening and monotonous process. All of America watched the growing figures in the little boxes over the shoulders of the network news anchormen. We were all aware that this was not a baseball score. These were not runs or points but human lives— in some cases, our neighbors and friends, in some cases, our very own sons. If this were all the television networks had done, I'm convinced it alone would have brought an end to the war. But the media did more. We saw the anguish on the faces of children burned by napalm. We heard the screams of wounded soldiers, not in some staged drama, but in real life. We even saw a man hold a revolver to the head of his bound victim and pull the trigger. Liberals and conservatives alike became sick of the war, and we each developed our own rationale for getting out of it.

Yet, we conservatives have not been able to raise public consciousness and media concern to win the war against drug and alcohol abuse. Consider only this statistic: for every young American who died in that horrible, longest war in America's history, *two* Americans will die every year, either directly or indirectly, because of alcohol abuse. Thirty thousand a year will die of cirrhosis of the liver, five thousand as a result of alcoholism or alcoholic psychosis. Accidents, homicides and suicides related to alcohol will take the lives of sixty thousand. Just picture your favorite evening newscaster with the little box in the background over his shoulder: "Another two hundred sixty dead today."[12]

I've only been talking about deaths. These figures don't begin to measure the full casualty count—the wounded. For every one of the twenty-five thousand alcohol-related highway deaths per year, there are hundreds, perhaps even thousands, more who survive and suffer. They are widows and orphans and quadriplegics. A government report states flatly that alcohol is responsible for 60 percent of all child abuse, for 80 percent of all home violence.[13] Fetal alcoholic syndrome is now the third major cause of mental retardation due to birth defects in this country.[14] And, though it can't compare with the cost in human tragedy, alcohol causes $27 billion in direct damages each year.[15] The death rate, staggering as it is, only begins to tell the story.

If all these statistics could be personalized, if we could get to know the disfigured cheerleader and meet the well-respected professional in our community who ran her down, if we could find the name of the judge who put him back on the streets within twenty-four hours, then perhaps we would be moved enough to put the problem on a front burner and try to solve it.

While the solution is elusive, we have stumbled onto some approaches. For example, in 1978, only a year after Michigan raised its minimum drinking age, it experienced a 31 percent reduction in alcohol-related automobile accidents.[16]

Yet liberals often oppose conservative ideas such as stiff penalties for drunk driving, or raising the minimum drinking laws. They consider such efforts as moralistic—more examples of conservative attempts to impose our values on society.

As staggering as America's alcohol problem may be, the abuse of drugs poses an even greater danger, even though the numbing statistics of alcohol use would actually look worse. Drugs are more threatening because of the ominous fact that chemical abuse prompts only more chemical abuse.

Approximately 15 percent of our American population is prone to alcoholism. The other 85 percent might be spared by such things as tougher laws or abuse-awareness programs. Their habits and attitudes can still be changed. On the other hand, drug dependency or complete addiction can happen to anybody, not just 15 percent of the populace. Once caught in the drug trap, users appear to have no easy way out. The numbers don't fluctuate, they only go up. Knowing of the harmful effects, even knowing that drugs ultimately mean death, has not stopped the user.

How large will the numbers have to get before all of American society—not just government, but the artists, the entertainment industry, business leaders, the sports world and the media—become truly serious about solving the problem? Will we be too late? Are we already too late?

The web of degradation brought on by drugs pulls in otherwise honest citizens, even large corporations and banking institutions, which often sell out to the illegal drug industry because the profits and stakes are so large.

Because drug dealing is illegal, the billions of dollars it generates are not subject to government taxation or regulation. Since drugs are often grown overseas, an estimated one hundred billion dollars of untaxed money leaves the United States every year to purchase them—more than the huge amounts spent to import of our crude-oil energy needs! In 1982, it was estimated that the total spent on drug trafficking exceeded our own record trade deficit. The money (tax-free, of course, because it is illegal) then pours back into the United States, where it competes with honest dollars for real estate, stock, buildings and goods. America is being morally and economically ravaged, yet many in the Establishment seem quite willing to wink at drug use. There is an attitude of "let the kids have their fun," or, in the case of some artists and entertainers, "let's join them ourselves."

Another factor in America's frightening drug crisis has been the involvement of foreign powers and revolutionary organizations, including government funding of the industry in some not-so-friendly countries. While many in America seem quite willing to ignore the growing numbers who are chemically dependent, there are international forces that are glad to help the problem grow.

Alcohol is also big business. Yet the continual slaughter of innocent people on America's highways doesn't seem to arouse the power brokers of America or trouble the consciences of the politicians. Television programs suggest that many networks are quite sincerely committed to solving the nation's social problems, yet they apparently see no contradiction in glamorizing the use of alcohol and drugs. But America cannot afford to look the other way. Her population must stay physically and mentally alert. The times are too dangerous.

As one reviews our violent society, one cannot help wondering why. How could America, the land of the free, put its citizens at risk? How can Socialist countries and nations with dictators have less violence inflicted upon their people? Does freedom breed criminal conduct?

Something has gone wrong. Have we lost our moorings?

A LOSS OF ABSOLUTES

CHAPTER

8

Conservatives see a parallel between the secularization of American society and the increase in violent behavior. In recent years, liberals have freely challenged the moral absolutes and religious traditions at the very foundation of Western civilization, and they have showed little concern for what was left in their place. The result has been an increasingly amoral society.

Some liberals would deny that their legal decisions or legislation were intended to have any philosophical impact, only, perhaps, a political one. They are the objective watchdogs, liberals say, carefully monitoring the moralists, religious or otherwise, who seek to impose their way of life on others. They see as the most immediate threat the "new religious Right," with its agenda of reestablishing traditional family values and prayer in schools and prohibiting federally funded abortions.

It is true that there are religious overtones to the modern conservative movement. Coinciding with its rise has been a spiritual renewal among the general American population. Many Jews have rediscovered their own orthodoxy, and Christian youth have awakened to their faith. No one can say for sure whether all this is a reaction to and an indictment of the liberal Establishment and the meaningless amoral drift that the country has taken. What is seldom realized, however, is that liberals have also based their politics on religious faith. The modern liberal political movement of the twentieth century followed its liberal theological forerunner.

THE SOCIAL GOSPEL

With the industrialization of the United States in the mid-nineteenth century, American churchmen began to borrow heavily from the new philosophies and ideas of popular liberal German theologians. There were great discussions about what was called the "social Gospel." The rise of the cities brought problems American society had not encountered before—unemployment, urban crime and the poverty of the slums. Some churchmen were especially embarrassed by what they felt was the hypocrisy of religions that addressed the spiritual nature of man, but left him hungry or jobless.

The division of liberals and conservatives in the religious world soon spread into the larger culture. Liberals tended to come from the large cities, where they faced the problems of industrialization head-on, and where the universities and seminaries, with their new ideas, proliferated. Conservatives tended to represent rural America, the vast majority of the population at the time.

Of course, I am generalizing. There were many religious conservatives in the city, and some religious liberals in the country. Nevertheless, this cultural dichotomy partly explains why the modern political conservative movement of the 1960s sprang from rural and suburban America, and has only now begun to reach the ethnic and minority groups of the inner city, for whom many of us believe it has the most to offer.

For years, American religious conservatives, or traditionalists, were easily able to isolate the new liberal movement. Since the majority of the members of the Catholic church came from the cities, Catholics were able to see the problems that the liberals spoke about, and address them. Meanwhile, liberal Protestant churchmen were greatly outnumbered in their own denominations and had to content themselves with shocking essays or sermons to draw attention to the social issues. In a strictly political sense, the inner city was still at the mercy of an agrarian society. America was still on the farm. The newspapers, the Congress, the power Establishments of the time were very much traditionalists.

At this point, America was still very religious. There was not only prayer in schools, but teaching from the Bible as well. The popular McGuffey *Eclectic Readers,* in which ten-year-olds read Webster, Milton, Jefferson, Shakespeare and Bacon, were loaded with Bible verses. In the second edition, a typical question was, "What is the Fifth Commandment?" Some liberals must have grown quite frustrated with a society that prided itself on being so religious while it ignored the problems they felt needed urgent attention.

In time, the self-criticism within the organized religions of America led some liberal Jews and Christians to challenge the very orthodoxy of their faith. Some of the most critical and basic doctrines were held in contempt. Some Christian theologians questioned the virgin birth, for example. Liberal Jews questioned the relevance of their laws in a modern age.

This was not unique to America. If anything, America was quite behind the times. This great theological and philosophical war had already been waged in France. Eighteenth-century French philosophers had taught that liberty and religion were natural enemies. The church had defended the monarchy. Similar philosophical and religious battles were to break out across Europe. Always the church defended the state, preaching the "divine right of kings" and quoting the admonitions of Saint Paul to respect those "in authority over you." This process had continued through two centuries, until the czar was overthrown in Russia. The Marxist Peoples' Revolution vanquished the last great autocracy from the continent.

In 1831, the famous French jurist, Alexis de Tocqueville, visited the United States. He soon became the European authority on American culture and politics. Tocqueville was surprised at the vital role that religion played in the new nation. He wrote, "Religion in America takes no direct part in the government of society, but it must be regarded as the first of their political institutions. . . . I do not know whether all Americans have a sincere faith in their religion, for who can search the human heart, but I am certain that they hold it to be indispensable to the maintenance of republican institutions. This opinion is not peculiar to a class of citizens or to a party, but it belongs to the whole nation and to every rank of society."[1]

Tocqueville's observations were not well received in Europe. It had taken philosophers and political revolutionaries many generations to break free of the domination of church-backed governments. The American experiment, thanks to the wisdom of our founding fathers, made sure that government endorsed no single religion, but rather encouraged them all. Said Tocqueville, "The philosophers of the 18th century explained in a very simple manner the gradual decay of a religious faith. Religious zeal, said they, must necessarily fail, the more generally liberty is established and knowledge diffused. Unfortunately, the facts by no means accord with their theory. There are certain populations in Europe whose unbelief is only equalled by their ignorance and debasement, while, in America, one of the freest and most enlightened nations in the world, the people fulfill with fervor all the outward duties of religion."[2]

Eight years after *Democracy in America* was published, Karl Marx's *Das Kapital* was released. While it was primarily an account of economic theories, Marx nevertheless jumped into the debate, calling religion "the opiate of the people," characterizing it as primarily a political tool for the establishment to keep the masses in line.

In the United States, the issue of slavery threw the whole liberal-conservative religious debate into confusion. Liberal and conservative churchmen took both sides of the issue. In the North, the church pulpits blazed against the indignity of enslaving other human beings. In the South, the church defended it with Saint Paul's admonition for Christians not to resort to violence, but to live peaceably under whatever government is in power: "Slaves, be obedient to your masters."

The American Civil War speeded up the process of industrialization. The population of the cities exploded, and, correspondingly, their political power grew. The "social Gospel" became an issue in every major American Christian denomination.

Meanwhile, in Europe, the German philosopher Friedrich Nietzsche was declaring flatly, "God is dead." To Nietzsche, modern man had created his own god on paper, just as surely as primitive man had created gods of stone or wood. Nietzsche proclaimed that traditional religions would remain for a while as a necessary crutch for the ignorant masses, while the elitists and the intelligentsia could move on to the realities of life.

In the United States, the liberalization of our educational process was well under way. In 1857, the McGuffey *Eclectic Readers* had been taken from the schools for a substantial rewrite. Shortly after the Civil War, they were withdrawn altogether.

THE LIBERALS SEARCH
FOR TRUTH

It is fair to say that the American liberal religious movement of the nineteenth century, and even the political movement that followed in the early twentieth century, manifested no conscious desire to impose its own fixed doctrines or philosophy of life on American society. In fact, it had none—at least, none that could unite all liberals under a common banner.

In its most subtle form, American liberalism said in effect to the church and later to the government, "Stop teaching your values. We're not saying you're wrong. We're just not so sure you are right about everything, and we want to discuss it without resolution." This didn't seem like an unreasonable argument at the time, but with hindsight, we can see its destructive result. The conservatives failed to recognize the attack and did not fight back.

Christianity had grown soft from the lack of internal criticism. It had arrogantly enjoyed so many centuries of temporal power that it was not accustomed to responding to questions raised by a scholar tucked away in a university. The church saw itself as the financier, the patron, even the original organizer of the educational process. It did not feel compelled to answer all the questions that were raised. And when the church did finally deign to discuss issues and faith, its answers were often illogical, weak or even irrelevant.

In 1925, the liberal and conservative religious movements collided in a Tennessee courtroom. A young schoolteacher named Scopes had violated Tennessee state law by teaching Darwin's theories of evolution. Brought in to assist the prosecution was the flamboyant Democratic presidential contender, William Jennings Bryan, an outspoken fundamentalist Christian whose political career was most famous for its populist, grass-roots support. Representing the defense was one of America's most famous and talented criminal attorneys, Clarence Darrow, a longtime foe of organized religion. Darrow believed that "crime is a social disease that should be cured, not punished."[3]

At issue was not whether the doctrine of evolution should take the place of the Biblical account of Creation. The question was whether the theory of evolution could be discussed at all, whether it could even be mentioned in the classroom. Interestingly enough, Scopes lost the trial; Darwin's theory could not be taught in the schools. But the result was a national public rebellion. Censorship was as wrong then as it is now. We believers in the Old Testament want the theories of both evolution and Creation taught.

We modern conservatives are not afraid of discussing all the possibilities of unproven theories. Unfortunately, in many school systems, the liberals have now censored the teaching of Creation. Yet is censorship by liberals right and by conservatives wrong?

When the modern liberal political movement was born in the 1930s, there was still no conscious intention of supplanting America's Judeo-Christian culture. Indeed, Franklin D. Roosevelt, the first truly modern liberal president, ordered the government to give away New Testaments to members of the armed forces.

In America, at that point, the philosophical liberal only saw himself as being open, willing to learn and, above all, curious about the truth. He thought of himself as a scientist, willing to experiment with thoughts just as his liberal political counterpart was willing to experiment with government policy. There is no doubt that many liberals resented what they saw as the narrowness and absoluteness of religion. Most of their ideas came from a European tradition that had included long centuries of political domination by state religions. The liberals resented the simplicity with which the church and the synagogue dealt with complex questions of life. But they saw it as more ignorant than harmful.

By the end of World War II, it was becoming increasingly clear that the liberal theological movement had shifted its purpose. It was, in fact, not really religious at all, insofar as religion implies a Supreme Being. A great many liberal theologians had long since rejected the concept of a personal God.

Let me add a note of caution at this point. It is perfectly legitimate for me to refer to the American theological debate of the nineteenth century as liberal versus traditional or orthodox. It is perfectly accurate for me to refer to the liberal philosophical movement. I am simply using the same terms that historians use when describing these events. Yet not all liberal movements are the same. For example, there are some movements that would be liberal in the context of one religious or social constituency and very conservative in another, or even conservative compared with society in general.

Let me add one more disclaimer. Many liberals would not appreciate the lineage I am attributing to their political philosophy. There are political liberals who are very conservative in their personal life-style and faith. They embrace liberal political doctrine precisely because they believe it is the fairest and most consistent with what their faith teaches them about life. If they are Christians, they are pro-choice or against school prayer because they do not wish to see the church regain a temporal power that it abused in past centuries and should never have had in the first place. If they are Jews, they see the very antagonism that liberals have against organized religion as their best guarantee that they will not be intimidated by a majority religion or intolerant government.

Then there are the liberals who become conservatives precisely because of the social issues. American Catholic bishops, very much inundated with European concepts of economics and history, can sound extremely naive when discussing the American free-enterprise system. Very few have any appreciation of conservative fiscal theories and how they work for the laboring class. However, they have become politically conservative because they see the movement as the best way of guaranteeing the sanctity of life and stopping federally sponsored abortions. They would certainly not appreciate an account of liberal politics that shows its roots in Nietzsche and even farther back in the French Revolution.

Finally, there are atheists or agnostics who are conservatives in spite of the theological and Judeo-Christian roots of the movement. They simply see conservatism as the best way to deal with crime, or to unleash the full productivity of the work force, or to deal with foreign powers. So keep in mind that I am only describing the evolution of political movements. They have attributes unique to themselves, but not binding on their individual members.

By the 1940s, the American liberal philosophical movement passed beyond the theological debate that had raged a century before. In its own mind, it had won the argument with Jews and

Christians. Therefore, the liberal philosophical movement had no legitimate reason to exist, if it were only to continue to be antireligious. This was the time to be positive, to offer some explanations of its own. For even if liberals felt comfortable rejecting the answers that the Jewish and Christian faiths offered, they could not as easily put aside the great questions those religions raised. Man's whole purpose for existing was, to the liberal, suddenly ambiguous. Was it to serve only God, only man or both? The intellectual vacuum was great.

It was at this time that existentialism became quite popular. Though it could trace its roots to Kierkegaard, and perhaps even to earlier thinkers, it was the modern liberal French philosopher, Jean-Paul Sartre, who became most identified with the movement. Sartre, who also toyed with communism, eventually became the rage on liberal college campuses in America and Western Europe. Though many of his followers found themselves sympathetic to the worldwide Socialist movement, radical Marxists were threatened by the popularity of existentialism. Those very revolutionaries whom Sartre romanticized were quick to burn the philosopher's books when they assumed power. They didn't want anyone challenging their authority.

THE HUMANIST MANIFESTO

In 1973, two hundred educators, philosophers, government officials and political activists signed the *Humanist Manifesto*. Among the more famous signatories were Jimmy Carter's secretary of education, Shirley Hufstadler, and Walter Mondale's brother, Lester. Pledging to rid society of injustice and bigotry, the document, among other things, calls for a stricter separation of church and state. However, its major thesis is that man is the measure of man and not subject to any higher authority. We conservatives reject this man-centered philosophy. (Let there be no mistake about the modern meaning of terms. Humanists espouse a man-centered and a man-measured philosophy; humanitarians serve mankind; humanities are the study of literature, philosophy and art. We conservatives embrace the last two and oppose the first.)

As a philosophy, humanism is not as intellectually consistent or as systematic as existentialism, but as a representation of liberal thought, it is much purer. The modern humanist believes that human beings can attain self-fulfillment and ethical conduct without resorting to supernatural religions. Humanists describe themselves as nontheistic.

Long before the manifesto was signed, humanist concepts began to appear so routinely in school textbooks and governmental policies that conservatives began complaining. Liberals, we charged, were doing the very thing they feared we would do, namely, using the government to promote a specific code of conduct and morality. Only now there was an added twist. Since humanism was nontheistic, its values were promoted without appearing to violate the separation of church and state. On the one hand, we charged, the government was using its power in an unprecedented way to inhibit the influence of religion. On the other hand, it was shamelessly advancing a philosophy of humanism. In several court cases, conservatives tried to prove that humanism was itself a religion and, thus, must abide by the same rules. But this strategy didn't work.

It is true that most liberals did not personally consider themselves humanists, just as many conservatives were not necessarily Orthodox Jews or fundamentalist Christians. Nevertheless, conservative political attitudes reflected Judeo-Christian roots and a belief in absolutes. And liberal politics, whether most liberals were aware of it or not, reflected the new humanistic movement.

This situation caused some rather awkward political and moral contradictions. There were liberal politicians, for example, who insisted that they were personally against abortion, but, rather than burden the general public with their view, they would continue to support the government's policy of sponsoring abortions with taxpayer's money. Likewise, not a liberal politician could be found who would admit that he enjoyed seeing movies depicting teenagers cut apart by chain saws. Nevertheless, local communities' attempts to ban the popular violent motion picture, *The Texas Chainsaw Massacre,* or any other violent motion picture, were stiffly resisted. Conservatives were accused of "censorship." No liberal public figure would dare indicate anything but disgust at the controversy surrounding the nude photographs taken of Brooke Shields as a child without her permission. Nevertheless, a liberal Supreme Court refused to consider the actress's attempt to stop publication. The First Amendment, as liberal jurists interpreted it, guaranteed Americans the right to see those pictures.

Often, the rationale behind these stances was inconsistent. But always, the liberal position and, eventually, the government's position, coincided neatly with modern humanism. In the case of abortion, liberals invoked all the high-sounding democratic rhetoric they could find. In a democratic society, we must allow the majority to work its will, they told us, even when that will is personally repugnant to us as individuals. Citing polls that show a majority favoring legalized abortion, liberals insisted that women be given "free choice."

Students who wished to pray in school, however, should not be given free choice. Dismissing polls that showed an overwhelming majority of Americans favoring such a privilege, liberals went so far as to prevent even a moment of silence at the beginning of a school day. This time, it was the minority we must respect, said liberals, those students and offended parents who held no belief in God.

In the 1980s, many frustrated conservatives began saying that it was neither the majority nor the minority to whom we were all paying homage. Nor was it the Constitution of the United States. Rather, it was a liberal philosophy of government that changed the rules to suit its own political ends. We were forfeiting our freedoms to conform to a humanistic philosophy that was patently antireligious.

That specter brought many new converts into the conservative camp. Some Catholic bishops, graduates of a liberal educational Establishment both in this country and in Europe, often equate compassion with socialism, and fail to appreciate the ethic as well as the efficiency of a productive society. Nevertheless, even though they retain their liberalism in other matters, the priority of social and moral issues has prompted some of them to become articulate conservative spokesmen. Jews have often suffered at the hands of majority religions in other lands, and find comfort in liberal themes of "separation of church and state." Still, the casualness with which the government resolves moral questions that have been debated for centuries—the fifteen million abortions in ten years, the genetic experimentation, the rash of mercy killings in American hospitals, a new generation of doctors with their glib theories of euthanasia, the glorification of violence in our cinema and art, the rise of crime—is beginning to make a lot of people in the Jewish community nervous.

A NEW GENERATION

For conservatives, the biggest question is how this loss of absolutes will affect a new generation. If the liberal Establishment is enforcing its philosophical bias, what chances do conservatives have to impart their values to their own children?

The policy guidelines for the government's family planning program are a case in point. After the epidemic of illegitimate births to unmarried teenagers, the program was directed to freely distribute birth control pills to minors. When the modern conservative movement developed enough muscle to elect its own president, it demanded that, at the very least, the government should inform parents when it was offering advice to their minor child and handing out pills that were, after all, prescription drugs.

Liberals were indignant. To them, this was just one more example of conservatives' "meddling," seeking to impose their sense of morality at the expense of the freedom of these young girls. This reaction was at once defensive and arrogant. It was defensive because liberals knew just how reasonable and logical the conservatives' request would sound to the general public. It was arrogant because a liberal Establishment knew that even a conservative president in the White House would not win against an entrenched liberal bureaucracy that, after years of power, was accustomed to running Washington and the country the way it wanted.

The liberal argument began by agreeing that a change in policy to notify the parents might possibly work for a well-to-do suburban family. But what about the neglected children of the inner city? That was where illegitimate births were so numerous. The very patronizing attitude of the liberals was that poor or minority parents tended to care less for their children.

Keep in mind that the conservative policy amendment would not have trampled on the rights of parents or teenagers with more liberal sexual attitudes. Confronted with a notice from a government agency that their daughters were receiving birth control pills, those "broad-minded," "liberated" parents could call their daughters in and tell them that their sex lives were their own business and that they should go out there and do their own thing.

Yes, it is true, some mothers might have simply thrown the notice in the wastebasket. But there would have been others, in both the suburbs and the inner city, who would have sat down with their daughters and shared their own values. Parents might have conveyed a religious conviction that had served them well in their youth. Or they may only have reminded a daughter that illicit sex has emotional and psychological ramifications. Since the whole idea was to avoid unwanted pregnancies, what would have been so wrong about involving the parents in the process?

But the latter possibility concerned the liberal politicians. Some parents would indeed have used the occasion to impart philosophical or religious values. That was what the conservatives hoped, but the "liberal watchdogs" wanted to be sure that the government apparatus was not seized by moralists. They wanted the government to provide services to people without making statements about right or wrong.

Yet that is exactly what the liberal Establishment itself has been doing all along—making statements on morality. Every government pronouncement has moral, immoral or amoral implications. When a thirteen-year-old girl is told that she cannot drive until she is sixteen, that she is not responsible enough to vote until she is eighteen, and that, in many states, it is against the law for her to drink a drop of alcohol until she is twenty-one, what kind of message is the government sending to her by offering her birth control pills free of charge? What is the purpose of the pills, unless the child is sexually active? And, if being sexually active were dangerous or risky or unwise for a child, then wouldn't the same government that denies her the privilege of driving an automobile say so?

Most damaging of all, when the government announced to the child that "your parents will never know," it not only had the effect of legitimizing sexual activity among unmarried teenagers, it also suggested that any parental objections or sermonizing should be ignored. The credibility of parents and their values were seriously eroded by the heavy hand of government.

In retrospect, the liberals were correct to have been both defensive and arrogant. They were right to have been arrogant because they did, indeed, win. The government would continue to pass the pills whenever a bureaucrat decided it should, without the permission or the knowledge of a minor's parents.

But liberals were right to be defensive as well. The liberal Establishment is clutching the levers of power more tightly than ever as the debate between conservatives and liberals has become much more liberal. The conservative movement is growing more popular with the general public, but it has a long way to go. Each little skirmish the conservatives lose helps define how radical the liberal Establishment has become, and how philosophically and intellectually exclusive it is. The liberal leaders have shifted the debate so far to the Left that they have abandoned many of their previous followers. People who are calling themselves conservatives today would have never dreamed of doing so even five years ago. Thus, the conservative movement grows stronger.

RELIGIOUS FREEDOM?

To defend their positions, both liberals and conservatives point to the First Amendment of the Constitution: "Congress shall make no laws respecting an establishment of religion, or prohibiting the free exercise thereof." Conservatives charge that the pendulum has swung so far that the government has become actively humanistic and antireligious.

When a liberal court decided that it was against the law for the Ten Commandments to be posted in a Tennessee classroom, or for a student to pray over his meal in a public school cafeteria, it was going beyond the principle of separation of church and state. The liberal court was suggesting that religion and all of the ethical and philosophical questions it raised may be dangerous to a free society. Why else would a document so historically and culturally rich as the Ten Commandments be banned from a classroom? At the same time, the Supreme Court determined that it was against the law for schools to allow a moment of prayer at the beginning of the day. What about silent prayer? No. Then what about just a moment of silence? No, the courts determined. That, too, would be "dangerous" to children's religious freedom.

Outlawing prayer in schools, which had been unchallenged by the finest American jurists and legal minds for more than a century and a half, was one thing. Rewriting history was another. A workman at Mount Vernon described the confusion and bewilderment of public school children who encountered the monument marking Washington's burial place. There was Holy Scripture engraved in stone, quoting the words of Jesus. The children were surprised to see such words associated with our nation's founder. So efficient has been the secularized, rewritten version of American history that the few public places where our ancestors can speak to us in their own words and in the context of their own values are those places where their words are engraved in stone.

Early American speeches, from Washington's to Patrick Henry's, have been detheologized in history textbooks.[4] No one has called it censorship. By the time modern conservative scholars compared new American textbooks with original speeches and filed their protests, it was too late. The erosion of American values and absolutes had already been underway for many years at the hands of the courts and scholars.

The American educational Establishment, its political infrastructure and its curriculum have been controlled by the liberal Establishment. Many conservatives—in fact, a huge number—pulled their children out of the public school system. By the 1970s, there were millions of students in private schools, where their parents thought they were beyond the reach of the federal government at last.

That has proved to be a naive hope. With the increase in government expenditures for education, personal property has been taxed to the hilt. Contrary to the public's perception, most parents of private school students have only average or below-average incomes. They suddenly found themselves in the position of paying for their child's education twice. There has been a people's tax rebellion to try to stop this process, to no avail. Even attempts by a conservative president to offer tax credits for private monies spent for education have been successfully resisted by liberals in the education lobby and their politicians.

In spite of the financial struggles of the private schools and the parents of their students, enrollment has continued to climb. While the typical new private schools frequently do not have science labs or gymnasiums, their graduates have regularly outscored the public schools on scholastic aptitude and achievement tests and on college entrance exams. In fact, educational quality measured by any standard has been accelerating consistently in private schools, even as it has been declining in public schools.

The liberal struggle for greater control of the education of our young shifted to a battle over teachers' certification in several midwestern states. After hearing both sides of the argument, liberal courts contended that students could not attend private schools whose teachers were not certified by the state. Schools were ordered closed. Results of the teaching and the students' achievements were not considered—only teachers' certificates from the state. Ministers who continued to operate schools were eventually arrested. In these cases, the private religious schools complained that they were in a no-win situation. How could they hope to build a value-oriented educational infrastructure when they were forced to hire teachers whose credentials conformed to the very system they were seeking to replace?

One of the most explosive questions in the private as well as public school systems concerns the teaching of life-styles that are contrary to the basic views of the Judeo-Christian tradition. This severe problem began when homosexuality was allowed to be taught as an alternative life-style in some public schools. Many Jewish and Christian parents were troubled. They saw homosexuality as a sin, not as an alternative. They were not insisting that public schools teach a Judeo-Christian philosophy of human sexuality to explain to students the wonder and joy of sex accompanied by commitment, but they were stunned that the educational process would so blatantly proselytize others with controversial theories.

New conclusions about homosexuality were advanced, and then surveys and scientific studies were produced to confirm them. Overnight, homosexuality was declared "normal." What science had for centuries said about the subject was dismissed with surprisingly little debate. It was censorship at its ugliest. Students were told to ignore what their own library books said. The changes came faster than the books could be published. While true scholars wouldn't make such leaps, they were all good enough to be passed off on high schoolers.

THE ULTIMATE TRAGEDY

The evidence is coming in. The modern humanistic values foisted off on the country are being measured. The liberal Establishment's value system is a failure. A report issued in 1984 by twenty-seven prominent liberal and conservative educators and citizens warned of a "serious decline" in character among our youth. The report pointed to an 800 percent increase in illegitimate births since 1940.[5] There were three times as many teenage homicides, and the suicide rate among youth, ages fifteen to twenty-four, has tripled since 1955.[6] The National Center for Health Statistics estimated that there were more than six thousand suicides in 1983 alone. The new sociological phenomenon was teenage "cluster" suicides. Within three months in 1984, six teenagers committed suicide in Clear Lake, Texas. At about the same time, there were eight in Plano, Texas. Over a two-year period, more than thirty teenagers took their lives in Westchester County, New York.

Another alarming new trend has been the epidemic of venereal disease. The American Social Health Association estimates that twenty-seven thousand cases are contracted every day.[7] Venereal disease will strike one out of every four Americans between the ages of fifteen and fifty-five at some point in his or her life. The annual health care bill is in excess of $2 billion.

Faced with these dismaying phenomena, conservatives are frustrated by how liberal moralists self-righteously use their power to prevent and root out any religious influence in society. Even as a new generation of American youth suffers to an extent never before known in this country, liberals stir up fears against the "new religious Right" and speak ominously of the dangers that its ideas pose.

Tocqueville observed that "while the law permits the Americans to do what they please, religion prevents them from conceiving and forbids them to commit what is rash or unjust."[8] He saw a beautiful balance in America. To restore that balance, we must allow for the freedom of all religions to teach and set examples without fearing a hostile government that opposes religious influences on society.

BIG BROTHER KNOWS BEST

However, we have come right back to Nietzsche and the European philosophers who believed that the "superior race" or "superior people," not the individual citizen, should make the decisions for society. Whether the subject is criminal justice, abortion, violence or alcohol and drug abuse, the elitists among us have taken on the great issues of theology and faith. These members of the liberal Establishment have distorted the First Amendment and seek to centralize government power in order to exercise social and economic control over the "ordinary" individual. We conservatives oppose this elitist dogma. We believe in the pluralism of "ordinary" people.

The elite Left seeks a humanistic, nonreligious society. They attack the integrity of religious institutions and leaders whom they regard as insincere or dangerous, all in the name of protecting the "ordinary people," who can't be trusted to make sound judgments. Just like their ruling counterparts in Marxist states, these elites will not tolerate religious pluralism or freedom unless dissenting institutions and their leaders can demonstrate some redeeming contribution to society as defined by the centralized power structure. These elites are essentially nonbelievers and have, therefore, decided on behalf of the rest of us that it is wrong to believe.

There is only one way out of this intolerable struggle, and that is to pick up the fight once more for religious tolerance and freedom. This time, there is no other shore to go to. The struggle must take place right here on the very soil where it occurred before, two hundred years ago. We conservatives must fight as hard and as persistent a battle for that portion of the First Amendment stating that "the Congress shall make no laws . . . prohibiting the free exercise of [religion]," as the battle for the wise prohibition against the "establishment of religion."

Conservatives, who for the time being are riding a wave of general popularity, must take on an entrenched elitist liberal Establishment. We must have the courage to effect change in power if we hope to stop the erosion of religious liberties and to recapture the values that have been at the very heart of the American spirit for a century and a half. It can be done.

We must awaken our consciences. We can revive the values that have guided previous American generations. Instead of fearing the role of faith in our society, instead of legally fighting it at every turn, we can set it free once again and enlist God's help to restore our national self-esteem.

WHEN CONSERVATIVES AREN'T CONSERVATIVE

CHAPTER

9

The president entered the room, took his seat at the table and announced, "Don Regan has an economic report to share with us. And then Dave Stockman wants to make some remarks."

Another meeting of the president's cabinet was under way. We had been gathering frequently in the White House to discuss the worsening economic news of 1982. "Reaganomics" was being blamed for the recession. It was not a fair charge, but that didn't slow the Washington media nor the liberals in Congress. The president was taking a terrible beating on the evening news and in the morning headlines. It made the attacks on me pale by comparison.

The calls for federal intervention to "prime the pumps" of economic activity were increasing in number and in decibels. Today's report from the secretary of the treasury concerned the alarming problems confronting the less developed nations that owed enormous sums of money to our privately owned banks. Secretary Regan was explaining the inability of those destitute countries to pay even the interest on the loans that individual banks such as Bank of America, Chase Manhattan and Citibank had made. The president was being told what actions the United States "must" take to salvage the situation.

After the Regan and Stockman briefings, there were several minutes of discussion before I asked, "Does anyone believe that these less developed countries will ever be able to pay back the principal on these loans?"

When no one spoke up, I asked, "If the loans are never going to be repaid, why should we again bail out the countries and arrange payment for their interest?"

The answer came from several voices at once, "If we don't arrange for their interest payments, the loans will go into default and it could put our American banks in jeopardy." Would the customers lose their money? No, came the answer, but the stockholders might lose dividends.

In amazement, I leaned back in my large, leather chair, only two seats from the president of the United States. I realized that nothing in the world could keep these high government officials from scrambling to protect and bail out a few very large and sorely troubled American banks. The president was given no options, no alternatives.

Would we have bailed out the corner drugstore if its owner made "mistakes of judgment"? Of course not. Nevertheless, it seems that if you are "big enough" when your company gets into trouble, a bailout program can be arranged. The owners of banks, railroads, savings and loan associations and airplane and automobile manufacturers have all been bailed out at various times in the past few years.

The politicians invariably talk about the jobs that would be lost and the upheaval that industry would experience. They act as if compassion for the investor dictates that the government should become involved on his behalf. What about compassion for the taxpayer, or the machine-tool operator who could not meet his expenses, or the failed filling station operator? Is this "selective compassion"? If a small businessman can fail because of "poor judgment," or "undercapitalization," or "changing technology," or "antiquated machinery or methodology" or "lack of efficiency," why not the big guys as well?

As I walked out of the White House that day, I thought of some of the men who had gone out of business in my hometown. A laundry—because a larger one in a nearby town could provide services more cheaply. An automobile dealer—because the population in our farm town was dwindling. A meat-packing plant— because it lacked the machinery and economics of scale. A small manufacturing plant—because new technology had made its product obsolete.

These adjustments to community life were taken in stride. Some who lost their jobs found others. Some had to leave town to find new work. Tough break? Yes. But none expected the federal government to bail him out.

When these facts of life come to a community, it hurts for a while—in some cases, for a long while. We have read stories about a military base being closed and thousands of people losing their jobs. While it wasn't easy for the jobless, we do not want the taxpayers to continue to finance what is no longer efficient or technologically outdated.

The government must not keep a military base operating just to maintain employment. Nor should the government use tax-payers' money for federal subsidies to any other form of business just to protect a way of life. Yet, that is what America is doing. Welfare for business must stop.

My little town is a ranching and farming community. As efficiency increases and technology improves, it has seen dwindling numbers of farmers on the irrigated flats, just as it has seen blacksmiths and the makers of wagonwheels and kerosene lamps squeezed out. It is sad but inevitable. As technology continues to improve and efficiency increases, others will have to sell out, too, and find something else to do. That is, unless the government continues to subsidize their existence.

FEEDING THE WORLD ON THE BACKS
OF AMERICAN TAXPAYERS

Rich, black dirt has made America one of the richest and most productive farming nations of the world. Unique geology has given us a marvelous bed of topsoil in our farm belt states and has allowed the farmers of our nation to aspire to the goal of feeding the world. But there are unavoidable realities of the marketplace that have been ignored.

American agriculture, when compared with that of any other nation in the world, has enjoyed incredible success. The commercial farms of this country have experienced rates of productivity and growth surpassing those of most other industries. This is true whether measured in terms of labor productivity or in terms of what economists call "total factor" productivity, which divides output by an index of labor, land and capital.

The same technology that gave the army its powerful tanks has given the grain farmer improved tractors that can pull multiple plows to turn the soil. Horses no longer sweat and lunge in contests to outhaul the neighbors' horses; rather, horsepower is now demonstrated in air-conditioned, self-propelled machines that combine several tasks in one turn around the field. Progress has converted horse barns to machine sheds.

Scientific advancements brought inexpensive fertilizers that increased the production on each acre of ground. It was no longer as necessary as it had been to rotate crops or rest the soil, since these modern fertilizers were replacing the elements that crops once robbed from the dirt.

Farmers who had bad years because of too much rain or not enough at the right time or blight or hail could not keep up. Smaller-acreage farms were wiped out and an entire year's work laid waste. Larger landowners whose holdings were scattered fared better against weather patterns and had the economic strength to buy out smaller farms. The seller began a new way of life, and the buyer became known as the corporate farmer.

Young men and women who liked the feel of the soil and the adventure of risk graduated from colleges armed with skills and knowledge in management and production. No longer were they just in farming; they were in agribusiness.

Where once a farmer had eked out a living, now owners of huge farms and ranches have integrated activities that change the land use and method of operation. The chicken coops have become row upon row of houses to raise fryers commercially. The small family garden patch has become a large field of lettuce or tomatoes. The old barn where the farmer hand-milked the cow every morning and evening has been replaced with a new, large building filled with stainless steel fixtures that can handle the continuous movement of cows through the mechanized milking system.

But because of this combination of advanced technology and increased productivity, fewer and fewer farmers are producing more and more of the foods and fibers for America. In 1930, employment in farming accounted for 20 percent of the labor force, yet by 1982, the numbers of farmers had dropped to an astounding 3 percent. The farming system, as a whole, has become more efficient, allowing the American consumer to pay the lowest food prices in the world. But farming as an industry is in trouble.

Despite the success and productivity of America's commercial farms, there is another side to United States agriculture—a tragic story of failed government programs, poverty on the small family farm and a crushing burden for the American taxpayer.

I have great respect and admiration for America's family farmers. They have been an American tradition, and their rugged pride has been a banner for this nation. One of the saddest realities in America is the phaseout of the small family farm. Because it has been for many scores of years the backbone of our nation, it is painful to think we may be seeing the end of the small-acreage farm. With its risks and rewards, with its ethic of hard work and wholesome values, the family farm has been plowed under by economic advances and by its long betrayal by the American government. Promises that have never worked and technology that has worked very well indeed have brought its hardship.

Inevitably, in the place of the family farm has arisen the corporate farm. Unless significant action is taken against government meddling in the marketplace, many more communities will suffer.

The farmers are doing everything they can, taking drastic steps to keep farms that, in many instances, have been in their families for generations. Traditionally, farm wives have worked beside their husbands. Only in the past couple of decades, with worsening conditions caused by governmental tinkering in agribusiness, have the wives had to find jobs off the farm.

Most farmers themselves have been forced to work other regular jobs, farming nights and weekends and using their vacation times to plant crops. They have no choice. Interest rates are too high, and commodity prices have not kept up with costs of living. Many of these same people who have worked the land with so much pride in order to feed America are now having to apply for food stamps.

Today, 12 percent of America's farms send to market about two-thirds of all farm products, for an average family income of over sixty-five thousand dollars. At the next level, 60 percent of all farms account for only 10 percent of total sales. However, note that this group of farmers derives only one-sixth of its income from the farms. Finally, the remaining 28 percent of farms produce about one-fourth of all farm product sales, while receiving about 60 percent of their income from the land. Thus, only about 12 percent of the farmers are fully dependent on agricultural activities; these commercial and corporate farmers do very well.

THE HELPING HAND
OF GOVERNMENT

Over the last fifty years, both conservative and liberal leaders have championed farm programs, which pretended to help the family farm and to bring price stabilization to the consumer markets. The rhetoric was attractive, but the results were a burden for the taxpayer and a loss of freedom for the farmers.

During that time, the number of farm units declined from about six million to about two-and-one-third million.

From the point of view of efficiency, this was not necessarily bad. But the overall result was the creation of strong, dominating political forces within the agricultural community. It was the ultimate vicious circle. Under the guise of fairness, increased productivity, stability and other "public good," these agricultural commodity groups with their political power sought favorable protection and treatment from the federal government. They got federal subsidies—a redistribution of wealth for their own gain, at the expense of the taxpayer.

Many will assert that the farm economy in the 1980s is in as serious a disarray as it was in the Great Depression of the 1930s. The irony is that those were the very days that spawned the agricultural programs that created the problems for the farmer and the taxpayer of today.

Those programs and their progeny resulted in $19 billion to $21 billion of federal spending in fiscal 1983, approximately equal to the value of net farm income in total. In addition, another $9 billion to $10 billion of harvested crops were paid out in 1983 to the farmers by the government in an ill-fated program called "Payment-in-Kind." At the same time, American farm exports dropped to $34.8 billion, down from $43.8 billion in 1981. The cost to the government in 1983 was about ten times what it had been in 1980, the last year of the Carter administration. The powerful political lobbies that protect the privileged position of certain segments of the agribusiness community seem to work their will regardless of which party controls the White House.

These loudly vocal groups, representing such interests as dairy farmers, the tobacco industry and the peanut farmer, have become unbelievably powerful. The parade of financial horrors inflicted by these groups on the American taxpayer seems endless. To the credit of the American Farm Bureau and other large, broadly based farm groups, they have not supported these programs benefiting special-interest groups. You may ask how these ill-advised, counterproductive farm programs became the law of the land. The answer is simply that politicians supported them without regard to the total farm picture—and with an eye toward their own reelection. Their interests and the interests of a segment of the farming community were put ahead of the public interest.

GOVERNMENT PRICE FIXING

Milk is the most political food in America. It has been the subject of federal programs for more than forty years.

Thirty years ago, each American consumed the equivalent of 350 quarts of milk and dairy products per year. Over the past twenty years, however, there have been substantial decreases in the consumption of butter, cream and plain whole milk. Today, per capita consumption in the United States averages about 260 quarts per year. In 1977, because the number of dairy farms had been rapidly decreasing over the last several decades and because the consumption of dairy products was on the decline, Congress (with the support of the administration) moved to stimulate dairy production.

Congress increased the price-support levels guaranteed to dairy farmers and tied them to an automatic, semiannual adjustment keyed to inflation. From the beginning of 1978 to the beginning of fiscal year 1981, the support level increased 40 percent. This, combined with low feed prices caused by the Russian grain embargo, resulted in the creation of new dairy farms, with old ones being enlarged and herds being increased. Everyone who could take advantage of the federal giveaway wanted to get his "fair share." In an agricultural economy staggered by double-digit inflation, the highest interest rates in a century and the Carter/Mondale embargo that singled out grain farmers, there were plenty of takers for the increased milk subsidies.

The result was a price-support system that cost the American taxpayers $250 million in 1979, growing to $2.2 billion in 1982, even though they consumed less milk. By fiscal 1983, the price tag had climbed to $2.5 billion, a tenfold increase in four years. What all this means is that American taxpayers were forced to pay $250,000 *each hour* to the government just to buy surplus dairy products.[1]

These unprecedented expenditures have left the government owning an enormous, growing stockpile of surplus dairy foods. As of June 1984, that astounding total included 355 million pounds of butter and 851 million pounds of cheese, as well as 1.38 billion pounds of dry milk, for which there is little market. The storage costs alone were over $127,000 *a day!*[2]

Sometimes the federal government's farm price-support programs discriminate between agribusiness groups themselves. Fifty years ago, the federal government set up a marketing order program that, in effect, provided government-sanctioned monopolies in California for Valencia oranges, almonds, lemons, raisins, Tokay grapes, dessert grapes, walnuts, dates, hops, prunes and navel oranges. Without any possibility of legal challenge, California growers are limited as to the quantities of these eleven crops that can be sold. They may grow as much as they want, you understand; they simply may not sell more of their product than the allocated quantity. The protectionist industry administrative committee members agree, by contract, to control the amount of produce that may be sold.

What happens is that a "privileged" orange grower in California has the protection of the government to keep prices high for consumers everywhere. Meanwhile, the Florida orange grower must fend for himself in the marketplace. Of course, since the whole transaction is sanctioned by the United States secretary of agriculture, there is no way the angry Florida grower can upset the deal by taking the matter to court.

Sometimes when Congress learns that agricultural programs haven't worked, their solution turns out to be even worse than the problem. One such program, which is also the largest, is called the Commodity Credit Corporation (CCC). In its simplest terms, the government supports agricultural prices and the incomes of farmers through loans and target prices, as well as programs requiring farmers to keep land out of production.

Under the loan program, farmers may put their crops in storage elevators and use them as collateral for low-interest loans from the government. The collateral has a specific value set by Congress. Corn, for example, is worth $2.55 a bushel. Or so Congress says. This program essentially provides a floor price for the commodity. Then, if the market price doesn't go above it, the farmer has the option of repaying the loan with his collateral. On the other hand, if the market price exceeds the value of his collateral, the farmer may sell it, repay the government, and pocket the difference.

In addition, there is a target price, set higher than the loan rates, which provides farmers a minimum return, or cost of production, on their commodities. The federal government makes up any difference between the market price and the target price with a direct "deficiency" payment to farmers.

From 1971 to 1980, these programs cost an average of $2.9 billion a year. With "conservatives" in control of our government in 1981, the Congress passed another farm bill that reauthorized and set payment levels for the various price-support programs. Because Congress assumed that inflation would continue, there was a proviso that the payments would increase automatically yearly for the next four years.

But inflation did not rise. Reagan's policies took effect and inflation was curbed. The automatic price increases continued unabated. Obligated to buy crops that farmers couldn't sell because of bumper crops in America and weak foreign markets, government expenses soared. In 1982 and 1983 alone, total expenditures of the CCC (which provides the price-support payments and the financing for exports) were larger than the total for the *entire decade* of the 1970s, over $30 billion! From 1980 to 1983, government payments to wheat farmers increased by 289 percent; payments to producers of feed grains (such as corn) rose by 430 percent; and payments to cotton farmers rose by 2,030 percent! Certainly the taxpayer is not benefiting from this program, and neither is the family farmer.

BAD TO WORSE

Because of the devastating failures of the 1981 congressionally enacted farm programs, the government acquired huge quantities of grain when so many of the farmers chose to take the federal loan money and give their stored grain to the government. With these increased government purchases, the storage fees alone amounted to tens of millions of dollars, and the prospects for additional quantities in 1983 forced the government to do something about it.

It adopted the "Payment-in-Kind" program, PIK for short. The idea was to exchange stored federally owned surplus crops for the promise that the farmers would allow their lands to lie fallow. They were supposed to sell the grain, giving themselves an income and disposing of the government's excess grain, thus cutting down on those horrendously expensive storage costs.

In actuality, what happened was that nearly $10 billion worth of PIK commodities given to farmers in 1983 kept about 48 million acres of America's farmland out of production, with disastrous side effects for hundreds of farm equipment stores and fertilizer and seed dealers. With fewer farmers buying planting supplies and equipment, many dealers had to close. It has been estimated that a quarter million jobs were lost in agribusiness and farm-related industries. PIK cost the United States economy billions in lost farm-export sales and could add another $20 billion to $30 billion to consumer food bills.

TO PLANT OR NOT TO PLANT

In 1930, the peanut farmers, who were planting about 1.1 million acres of land, asked for and received from the federal government rigid production controls limiting the amount of acreage that could be planted. These controls also guaranteed high subsidized prices with little regard for fluctuating world markets. In effect, the federal government's "guarantee of success" created an inheritable and valuable privilege for a select few.

Not many new farmers have been permitted into the peanut industry, and supply is controlled artificially without regard to market demand. Neither skill nor technology has greatly expanded the production of peanuts in fifty years. Today, about the same number of acres of peanuts (1.4 million) are grown by about the same number of farmers as in 1930. It is great for the privileged farmers, but it certainly hurts the taxpayer and consumer.

On the other hand, another group of farmers also joined together in 1930. They were also planting about 1.1 million acres of their crop—soybeans. These farmers did not ask the government for production controls. Instead, they believed that with a low, minimal price support, they could enter the free market and compete successfully. And they did. The consumer has benefited, as has the farmer, because today over 68 million acres of soybeans—a high-protein food helping to meet nutrition needs around the world—are harvested every year in America. Increasing numbers of soybean farmers have provided jobs for Americans, stimulating national and international economies. And their profits come from the marketplace, not government subsidies.

Something should be learned from this comparison. The free market does work, and acreage reduction or control programs do not.

A study of the past Department of Agriculture programs calling for acreage reduction is conclusive. Acreage-reduction programs do *not* reduce production in an economic manner. There are several reasons. First, farmers naturally take their worst land out of production and, with intensive farming and fertilization, till the remaining acreage for increased yields.

Second, farmers not in the acreage-reduction program expand their production, knowing that the government will try to support prices at high levels.

Third, while the United States tries to reduce its agricultural production, our foreign competitors continue to expand their production by using government subsidies. They export their surplus commodities and processed farm products to the United States.

Our government's policies have been based on the wrong premises. The potential for the production of food in the world has not been reached. The United States cannot control world food prices. As world food prices increase, new lands around the world are put into production, and enhanced farming techniques are used, such as fertilizers, insecticides and hybrid seeds. In addition, consumption patterns change. The demand for food is price-sensitive throughout the world.

The facts are abundantly clear. Over the long run, the United States government cannot successfully control the supply or prices of agricultural products, either domestically or internationally. Nor can the government guarantee the cost of production or a return on profit. Yet year after year, conservatives, as well as liberals, have ignored market realities in an effort to benefit special segments of the agriculture community. Neither the taxpayer nor the farmer can afford this irresponsibility any longer.

THE ROAD TO REALITY

For there to be success domestically and internationally, there must be a return to market realities. While this is easy to say, the self-interest of special-interest groups and the nearsightedness of both liberal and conservative politicians seeking to satisfy their loudest constituents will have to be overcome. It will take courage to espouse the logic of marketplace solutions. It will take even more courage to provide the leadership to establish them.

Congress must first give to the secretary of agriculture the flexibility to begin to return to the forces of supply and demand, along with the direction to do so. The selfish political interest groups will fight tooth and claw against this. Their privileged position has been sanctioned and approved by Congress for so long, they think it should be hallowed ground.

The road to reality will not be easy. Some of those farmers who bought high-priced land with an unrealistic debt load, expecting the government to continue propping up high artificial prices, will probably fold. With each failure, the politician will be tempted to choose a short-term expedient support system that will lead to long-term hardship in America.

So what can be done?

—Commodity credit loan rates must be lowered until market-clearing levels are found. Any future increase must then be tied to changes in the market.

—Because of world market conditions and the potential for large-scale crop failure or other such disaster, a loan program should continue. But it should be well below the market-clearing price so that the federal farm policies will not dictate or influence the allocation of farm resources or market activity. The approach to soybean production that I discussed earlier has been a real success and would be a good model for other crops.

—Target prices created by Congress to guarantee farmers the return of the cost of production plus profit must be frozen, reduced and then eliminated as a signal to producers that they must eventually live with the returns generated in the marketplace.

—The farm-held reserve of grain will have to be modified or eliminated so that it cannot be used as a backdoor approach to supply and price management.

—Production controls over land use should be totally eliminated. They do not work. Farmers simply use more and more sophisticated technology to increase yields on their acreage not taken out of production. Technology should be utilized wherever possible, but not to the detriment of the American taxpayer. The only success these expensive "acreage diversion" schemes have is in diverting billions of dollars from the pockets of taxpayers to the pockets of large landowners.

FOREIGN STRESSES ON AMERICAN FARMERS

What happens in Peoria has a dramatic impact on people in Pakistan and Peru. And, of course, the opposite is true. The linchpin of a market-oriented agricultural policy must be strong action on the part of our government to make certain our farmers are given a chance to compete fairly in international markets. Today, they are not.

Several European countries give heavy subsidies to their own farmers so their goods can be sent to the United States. And European countries are not the only ones violating our shores with government-subsidized, processed foods, meat and other agricultural products.

While our foreign "friends" are attacking our markets, they put up protective barriers to defend their own domestic markets. Even though countries like France and Japan may say all the right words about the values of free trade and swear that it is their policy, their deeds belie their words. Permits are denied, or unloading is delayed until our food rots on the wharf before it can even get to the marketplace. When our liberal State Department officials finally protest over tea or cocktails, they are assured it was all a mistake.

Our farmers are not being championed or defended in international trade. We should seek free trade, but there *must* be reciprocity. Regardless of what our foreign competitors *say* their policy is, we must reciprocate with whatever it, in actuality, is.

If they deny us their markets, our markets must be denied them.

It will take more courage than our timid government leaders have shown so far. But fairness must come. Our farmers deserve it. Now is the time for boldness and courage.

CREATING JOBS
IN JAPAN

CHAPTER

10

Conservatives favor an open domestic and international marketplace, but the fact is that free trade just does not exist in many places of the world. Major changes must be made if we are to protect our industrial strength and create the jobs needed in this country in the coming decades.

There was a time when we in the United States were able to compete on the basis of just our productivity and our quality of goods. We had an advantage in technology and machinery. Other nations simply couldn't match the speed at which we could turn out quality products. Today, all industrialized nations have access to the same equipment and technology (in many cases, because the United States government has financed them with American taxpayers' money). The bottom line is that manufacturing capabilities have been mostly equalized among several producing nations. The competitive edge for the world markets now goes to those who can produce at the best price.

Most of the nations of the world, if not all of them, have taken action, openly or secretly, to protect their key industries and their labor force, thus frustrating free-trade efforts. Because of soft currencies (money that is not acceptable in international trade) in the less developed countries, counter trade and barter have become more common today in international import-export activities. For example, when a South American country wants Caterpillar tractors from America and has no United States dollars to pay for them, it substitutes coffee beans, bananas and tennis shoes for dollars. Some experts believe that counter trade and barter already account for as much as one-third of all transactions. No one can deny they are a growing force that will work against free-trade commitments by restricting participants, prices and the other marketplace factors.

A further complication has been some foreign governments' practice of subsidizing their own industries. France and Japan, like many other countries, have supported selected domestic industries—for examples, processed foods and motorcycles. How big are the subsidies? It is very difficult, if not impossible, to follow the trail of tax supports or government regulations benefiting the favored businesses. Socialistic countries with government ownership conceal how much they subsidize into their industries' efforts to increase exports to the United States. Many experts believe that the subsidies are substantial. Private corporations in the United States, even the big and powerful ones, can find their products underbid and eventually pushed out of the domestic market altogether by a foreign competitor with its government's bankroll behind its product. And we frequently give Communist and Socialist countries "favored nation" status.

As another tactic against free trade, governments like that of Japan can make it very difficult, if not impossible, for us to ship our manufactured goods into their countries, even though some of their stated policies make it sound as if they support free trade. The American businessman is confronted with great resistance: red tape, delays in issuing permits, and difficulties in unloading merchandise and putting goods in foreign consumer markets.

In addition to government subsidies and interference in foreign lands, American business is handicapped by the costs of environmental protection and enhancement that it pays while foreign competitors do not. In recent years, the United States has wisely determined that protecting environmental values should be considered a cost of doing business. Unfortunately, a great many of our competitors, like Mexico, Canada, Japan and Korea, do not share this vision. Their environmental protection standards are not nearly as tough or as expensive as ours. So American industry is not only forced to clean up its own activity, but sometimes loses business and employment (jobs) to the foreign "dirty" producers.

Probably the largest disparity in the cost differential between American and foreign manufactured goods is labor. In this country, we have raised the quality of life so that health, education, housing, recreation and other standard-of-living measures are far higher than those in other countries. We do not want to sacrifice that high quality of life. But to keep it, we must have jobs.

According to the American Iron and Steel Institute, a steelworker in America in 1984 earned an hourly average wage of $24.07. In France, he earned $13.22; in Japan, $11.89; in West Germany, $12.91; and in Korea, he earned from $1.25 to $2.50 an hour. The difference is dramatic, and it has been a major factor in encouraging the shift of American jobs to foreign countries.

America is still one of the world's greatest exporters of food, war materials, airplanes, medicine, medical supplies and high technology. But other exports, such as our natural resources, we buy back in the form of labor-added and value-added goods. The United States ships scrap iron to Japan, for example, and it is returned in the form of cars. We send logs to Korea, and they come back as finished kitchen cabinets. We send cotton to Taiwan, and it returns as shirts and coats. American technology exported to Japan has been coming back to us in the form of cameras, television sets, stereos and radios. Most of America's trading partners purchase from us only what they need to produce goods that are then sold to us.

Some fear that America's greatest export in recent years has been jobs and profits to foreign competitors, creating domestic unemployment and economic hardship. Others brag about America's foreign trade, claiming that one in eight American jobs is involved in export. This is a misleading statistic. Counting only true exports, goods that leave our country and don't come back in one form or another, fewer than one out of every 100 to 125 workers is involved in exports.

United States unemployment is thought to be politically acceptable if it is less than 8 percent of the work force. But why should anyone who belongs to the 8 percent and *wants* to work be written off by the political process? It is our own government's policy that has created millions of jobs in Japan and unemployment in America.

In recent years, America's negative balance of trade has reached an annual high of over $100 billion. International trade is often a confusing subject to the layman. But anyone can appreciate the fact that if, over a period of years, more money goes out than comes in for the purchase and sale of goods, we will be in serious trouble. Well, folks, we are now in serious trouble.

SOLUTIONS NOBODY WANTS

To address the problem, liberal politicians have formulated what is called "domestic content" legislation. This approach would mandate that a certain percentage of legislatively identified products be manufactured solely in the United States. This would give assistance, perhaps even subsidy, to some industries while ignoring others that are also under attack from foreign competition.

Political power would be the determining factor, not economic forces. The resulting distortion in our economy would be very detrimental and end up costing jobs.

Import quotas and tariffs on specific commodities have been and are being used by our government and all other trading nations. But the problem continues to grow, and more jobs are lost.

Some conservatives argue that we should revise federal regulations. They would call for an overhaul, or at least a pruning, of the excesses of the Environmental Protection Agency, OSHA, MESA and other agencies. There are, no doubt, regulations that are excessive and burdensome and detrimental to the creation of jobs and increased trade. However, modern conservatives believe that proper government regulation is critical for our safety and environmental protection, and must be retained. It would be wrong to eliminate regulations just because they are costly or because competing nations don't have them. No one wants to go backward. Progress is, after all, the objective.

Some futurists have argued that it is good to "let the smokestack industries leave our shores." They suggest that factories that cause pollution are not as desirable as the high-tech industries and service organizations that they hope would replace them.

This is a naive judgment on two counts. In the first place, for reasons of military security and general economic health, the United States cannot afford to lose her industrial capacity. In the 1970s, we learned what it was like to be politically blackmailed by a few oil-producing nations. While total independence and complete self-sufficiency are unrealistic goals, it would be extremely dangerous to forfeit our manufacturing industries and their labor force. It is absolutely essential for the United States to maintain the capacity to produce steel, aluminum, copper and the other materials needed for a sophisticated society. In order to do so, we must have mining, smelting, fabricating and distribution facilities.

Second, if we allowed the "smokestack" industries to leave, the transition from an industrial to a service economy would be problematic. A nation's wealth is determined by its natural resources, agricultural potential and manufacturing capabilities. All other economic activities are service industries, dependent on those three basic elements. And when one basic industry is hurt, many service enterprises fail. For example, the textile industry has faced tough foreign competition for years. According to its trade association, if one thousand textile or apparel manufacturing jobs were lost to a foreign country, another one thousand jobs would be lost in the incredible list of businesses that follows: seventeen restaurants, thirteen grocery stores, eleven gas stations, six apparel shops, three automobile dealerships, two hardware stores, two automobile accessory stores, two drug stores, one sports store and one jewelry store.[1] The same story could be told about any of the other basic manufacturing industries.

The most absurd governmental response to the exporting of United States jobs has been "jawboning," which consists of government agency heads and sometimes academicians in their hallowed halls and ivory towers urging American workers to increase productivity so that foreigners won't take their jobs. That's easy to say, as long as you are not working on the factory line, in the steel mill or at the construction site. Only people who wear white collars and sit at desks can talk about the "easy" solution of increasing productivity.

Those who need to haul their goods are told by the government the maximum tonnage their trucks can carry, how many axles they may have and at what speed they can travel. Then they are told to increase their productivity.

Those willing to hire teenagers or the inexperienced are told by government or labor unions how old the applicant must be, how many hours he may work, how much money he is to be paid per hour and what jobs he may or may not have. Increase productivity? Those who want to manufacture certain products are, in many instances, told the quality that must be met, and the safety and environmental controls that must be maintained. Now, we all agree that compromising America's standards is not the answer. But government officials, congressmen and journalists who reduce the solution to improving the motivation of our labor force are incredibly naive. There must be bold action, and it can't wait.

DEPENDING ON UNCLE SAM

One of the secrets to America's great wealth has been her secure borders. During the critical period of the Industrial Revolution, America's two less powerful neighbors and the huge oceans that separated us from the world's great powers allowed us to prosper without the burden of great military expenditures.

Ironically, another secret was the British Empire. For more than a hundred years, Britannia ruled the waves—to be sure, usually in her own best interests. But even so, America benefited hugely because the sea-lanes of the world were open and regulated. Britain was not threatened by the growing economic might of America.

Today, the United States rules the waves, albeit in a much more modest sense. Our country and its military might keep the sea-lanes open and provide stability for the world markets. History is repeating itself, only this time with us in the British position, and the Japanese, who pay virtually nothing for our protection of them and their way of life, in the role of early Americans.

Our financial burden for defending the free world is staggering. American citizens and American corporations are taxed heavily for military defense, and even for military aid to our friendly but weaker allies. Seven percent of our gross national product is spent protecting ourselves and our allies—Japan, Germany, Korea, Taiwan, France and all the others. They, in turn, are freed from the need to tax workers and businesses to provide for their own defense. Japan invests less than two percent of its gross national product; Germany and France, four percent. Our military research and development budget is twice as large as the entire Japanese defense budget.

This tax burden for national defense also adds to the cost of American-produced goods and further handicaps our ability to compete in the world market.

We must now address the problem of America's staggering international trade deficit, which, if not soon corrected, will undermine the whole free world's economic and banking systems. We must seek to establish free trade and reciprocity. But conservatives must once and for all appreciate that free trade, as desirable as it is, is not being practiced by most countries. If other countries do not adopt free-trade practices, we must not allow them access to our markets. We must employ the same resolve that we muster when faced with any other kind of international crisis.

SHARE THE COSTS

I propose that a "market access fee" be assessed to each country seeking to sell its manufactured goods in America. The fee would not be assessed on each item imported, but on the governments. It would not be a return to the old tariffs that reward inefficiency and thwart the concepts of free trade. We would not charge countries exporting nonmanufactured goods such as bananas and coffee beans. But countries exporting manufactured products, such as automobiles, would be hit. The fees generated could be channeled into Social Security or unemployment benefits.

The annual "market access fee" that I propose would be determined by evaluating and adding three components:

1. An amount equal to the exporting country's fair share of the cost of defending the free world. This can be determined by comparing percentages of GNP spent on national defense and/or a per capita share of all free world defense budgets.

2. An amount equal to the pollution-control costs avoided by the manufacturing country. One must subtract the actual costs incurred from the costs that would have been incurred for environmental protection had the goods been manufactured here in the United States. This figure would be based on the volume of goods imported into America during the preceding year.

3. An amount equal to the wage differentials between the American working force and the exporting country's working force for the total amount of manufactured goods shipped to the United States in the preceding year.

America is the "world market" for manufactured goods. Few other countries have the money to purchase significant volumes of foreign goods. Not many Japanese automobiles are manufactured for export to Zaire, for example, and not many Korean-made machine tools go to Belgium. Not many Taiwan-tailored wool suits go to England; not many Swiss watches go to Japan.

America is *the* market. If these countries want to have access to our markets, let them share in the burden carried by our consumers and taxpayers. Our markets should be open to all who are willing to pay their fair share in championing world peace, protecting the environment and paying fair wages.

PART

III

THE DISARMING
OF AMERICA

CHAPTER

11

The original first ten pages of this chapter have been stamped Top Secret and are now in a vault under the command of one of the nation's leaders in military preparedness. Early in the administration, the president had asked me to participate in an "exercise" that proved to be one of my most interesting and eye-opening experiences during my tour of duty with the cabinet.

The several days I committed to this "exercise" took place in the greatest secrecy, classified at the highest level. As I was exposed to the briefings, information and procedures, it was easy to understand why. I was told not to tell even my wife about the "exercise." It was my first experience with anything like this, so I took my instructions very seriously.

A few days later, I was stunned to read about the whole affair in a leading newspaper and a weekly news magazine. The articles were written with remarkable factual detail. I spoke to White

House officials and to the general with whom I had worked. No one seemed to know, or would tell me, how such a story could get out. The articles didn't get a lot of national attention, and I wondered why. Maybe because truth is stranger than fiction and therefore wasn't recognized. Certainly the other side of the coin is more familiar—fiction made to appear like truth.

Because some of the information had been made public, I wrote a brief and breezy description of my experiences during that "exercise" to introduce this chapter.

I felt that if I didn't reveal anything that hadn't already been made public, I would not be violating any trust. But out of an abundance of caution, I sent the material to the proper authorities for clearance. (We conservatives are always cautious.) Within four hours, the general was on the phone telling me that my work had been classified Top Secret and now lay in his vault. I was ordered to destroy all copies and to erase the passages on the floppy disk of my word processor. I immediately complied, though I protested mildly. But he was adamant.

So I am now in the position of writing without being able to present some of the reasons for my deep concern for America's ability not only to defend herself and her allies but to advance the cause of freedom.

I can now appreciate the story that is frequently told about my former colleague in the cabinet, Secretary of State Alexander Haig. When General Haig was commander of all NATO forces in Brussels, he reportedly told a group of European businessmen as he opened his prepared remarks, "Gentlemen, if you understood what I know, you would agree with what I am about to say."

A LOSS OF WILL

In 1981, President Reagan inherited the problem of a dangerous deterioration in America's ability to defend herself and her allies.

Since 1974, when Southeast Asia had fallen and America had withdrawn to lick her wounds, the Soviet Union and its proxies had turned the world into one vast geopolitical playground.

Cuban armies ranged across Africa, from Ethiopia to Angola and Mozambique. Unchallenged, the Soviets toyed with one disruptive strategy after another. In the middle of the Ethiopian civil war, they suddenly switched sides. In 1980, when they grew frustrated with the Marxist prime minister of Afghanistan, the Soviets simply murdered him and his family in a bloody palace takeover, invaded the country with thirty thousand soldiers and brought in their own Czechoslovakian-trained Afghan national to serve as a puppet head of state.

The Soviets also established a foothold in Central America and blatantly expanded their bases in the Caribbean. In 1962, John Kennedy had taken us to the brink of a nuclear war when Khrushchev threatened to install missiles in Cuba, but in the late 1970s, America's defenses and willpower were so low that a Soviet-armed brigade camped ninety miles from Florida prompted little more than a protest by a few conservatives.

The most blatant example of what the Soviets and their Communist allies were capable of in the absence of American political-moral restraint was the subjugation of conquered Cambodia and South Vietnam in 1979. The Khmer people had barely survived the Chinese-backed Communist Pol Pot. According to the International Committee of the Red Cross, three million Cambodians had died between 1974 and 1979. Pot had been trying to impose his version of pure Maoist Marxism, which in his twisted mind called for the wholesale murder of teachers, writers, government officials, anyone who had served in the armed forces, anyone in the performing arts and all doctors and nurses.

When the Soviets backed a Vietnamese invasion of Cambodia, there was not much world reaction. Some Westerners decided it wouldn't hurt for the Chinese and Soviet proxies to fight it out among themselves. Others reasoned that because Pol Pot was the greatest criminal since Hitler, a little punishment was in order. First, the Vietnamese armies chased the black-pajamaed Khmer Rouge into the jungle. Then they set up shop in Phnom Penh, and Soviet advisers poured in. Within six months, the wholesale and systematic starvation of the Cambodian people by the Soviet-backed Vietnamese was underway. By most estimates, a million people died of starvation and disease in the early fall of 1979.

At first, the American liberal Establishment ignored this tragedy, which did not fit their post–Vietnam War scenario. During the reign of terror, documented reports and testimonies by the thousands came from Cambodia, but the *only* article in the American popular press appeared in *Readers' Digest.*

Meanwhile, from the former Republic of South Vietnam, news of other horrors began leaking to the West: massive economic and sometimes murderous reprisals against former government officials, soldiers, merchants, educators and anyone else who had been a part of the South Vietnamese establishment. The lucky ones were sent to "reeducation camps." American political conservatives had warned all along that this would happen. Defending peoples against such suffering was part of the moral rationale for American involvement in Vietnam. Liberals had promised that the mass murders that had occurred in the early Soviet and Chinese peoples' revolutions were no longer part of the Communist pattern. The North Vietnamese had kept their reign of terror under wraps as much as possible so as not to embarrass their American sympathizers.

Then came the waves of immigrants. The stories could no longer be ignored. An estimated two million boat people fled Vietnam, including many of the former Viet Cong leaders themselves. Truong Nhu Tang, the former minister of justice for the Peoples' Revolutionary Party, told the West that "never has any previous regime brought such masses of people to such desperation—not the military dictators, not the colonists, not even the ancient Chinese overlords."[1] Best estimates indicated that for every successful refugee, another died fleeing Southeast Asia.

Even the most conservative estimates put Vietnamese deaths by drowning or execution at five hundred thousand.

In October 1979, the genocide in Cambodia finally broke into the headlines. Three hundred thousand starving Khmer people had literally walked to the border of Thailand. It was a different time and place, and a different cause, but there was no mistaking the skeletal faces, the hollowed eyes with the same blank look, that had greeted American armies at Dachau. Thousands of miles away, American television viewers saw fields of skeletons with flies buzzing overhead. Afterward, liberal commentators, still clinging to their fantasies, tried to convince viewers that the Cambodians were starving because of Nixon's secret bombings nine years before.

While Americans argued among themselves about which of their policies had induced the Soviets and Vietnamese to do such terrible things, the starvation continued. World protests mounted month by month, until the Soviets finally decided that their great Vietnam War propaganda triumph over the Americans could be lost. In November, the Vietnamese sporadically opened the Cambodian port of Kompong Som and "generously" allowed the United States government, religious organizations and other Western nations to feed what was left of the starving Khmer people.

After a brief two-month respite, when the Western news media grew tired of the story and moved elsewhere, the Soviet-backed Vietnamese returned to their genocide. But, in the end, it was another Communist nation, not Western economic, political or military leverage that stopped the murder. For on February 17, 1979, the Peoples' Republic of China invaded Vietnam. With Vietnam absorbed by a war on two fronts, many Cambodians slipped into the jungles or crossed the border into Thailand where, even to this day, they continue to wage their war of "liberation" for the Khmer people.

In the middle of all this, back home in America, a new generation was riveted to its television screens, watching an NBC week-long drama on the Holocaust, asking their parents how such things could possibly happen, and why didn't somebody stop Hitler and help the Jews?

Meanwhile, the Khmer people, a race that had built a flourishing civilization thousands of years before Christ, was almost exterminated before our eyes. The American government had sat idly by. We could do little more than feed them, if and when their Soviet and Vietnam masters decided it was in their own propaganda interests to let us.

The United States had lost the will to impose its views on its own allies, let alone its enemies. By 1980, our conventional military forces were in tragic disrepair. Even the idea of nuclear parity was slipping. We were falling hopelessly behind in an arms race that we didn't want and, therefore, chose to believe wasn't happening.

In the late 1970s, President Carter began advancing his human rights program. But without any kind of a stick or military will, it was often exploited by our enemies. Somoza was undermined in Nicaragua, and the Sandinistas came to power. The Shah was undermined in Iran, and the Ayatollah Khomeini came to power. So despised was America's weakness and so misunderstood was its desire to encourage world disarmament that the Ayatollah arrogantly sanctioned a terrorist seizure of the American embassy and the holding of its employees as hostages. The impotent United States government could do little but try to negotiate through diplomatic channels.

When America did make up its mind to rescue the hostages, it used its most elite troops and its best equipment. The White House, once thought to be the most powerful place on earth, received hourly reports. But when the American troops came roaring over the Arabian Sea and into the desert, their helicopters began sputtering. Still halfway from their target, hundreds of miles into the desert of Iran, they broke down. There they sit to this day, rusting hulks half buried by the sand, monuments to a naive people so sensitive to their own imperfect use of power that they were apparently willing to forfeit it to madmen.

UNILATERAL RESTRAINT

How had America lost faith in herself, and how had she so easily let her power slip?

While running for president in 1960, John F. Kennedy had righteously alerted America to a "missile gap crisis." Some Pentagon experts were warning that the Soviet production of intercontinental ballistic missiles was outstripping our own. If the Soviets were not at that very moment threatening American nuclear superiority, they surely would be doing so very soon.

It was not an accurate assessment. While the Soviets had indeed begun to outproduce America in missiles, America's stockpile was far ahead. The Soviets had little chance of catching up. Still, the liberal Kennedy charged that Eisenhower and the Republicans had let things slip, a campaign issue that worked somewhat.

It is amusing to look back at this debate between a liberal Democrat and a moderate Republican. They weren't arguing about the need for American nuclear superiority. They were arguing over who could best get it. America still had that post–World War II national self-esteem and trusted her own use of power.

Winston Churchill wrote about those first few years after World War II when America was the only nuclear power: "No one in any country has slept less well in their beds because this knowledge of the atomic bomb and the method and the raw materials to apply it are presently largely retained in American hands. I do not believe we should all have slept so soundly had the positions been reversed, and if some communist or neo-fascist state monopolized for the time being these dread agencies."[2]

Compared with the coming bitterness of the Vietnam era, the Truman and Eisenhower years were a time of relative innocence.

Still, the seeds of political polarization had already taken root.
For one thing, liberals resented the demagoguery and extremes
of the Joe McCarthy hearings. And there was a growing uneasi-
ness with the power of the "military-industrial complex." Eisenhower himself first coined that phrase and warned it was not
in the best interests of the country to be frightened into buying
every piece of military hardware the Pentagon said it needed.

In 1961, President John Kennedy brought to his cabinet Robert
McNamara, who was typical of the liberal Establishment. He
had been the chief executive officer of the Ford Motor Company,
he was rich and he was idealistic. Kennedy and McNamara soon
concluded that there was no missile gap at all. In fact, they decided America was so far ahead that the Russians had given up.
"There is no indication that the Soviets are seeking to develop a
strategic nuclear force as large as ours," McNamara said.[3]

The new approach was unilateral restraint. The theory was that
the Soviet economy was so fragile, Kremlin leaders would wel-
come a halt in an arms race they knew they had already lost. And
what if Kennedy and McNamara were wrong; what if the Soviets refused to restrain themselves and kept on feeding their
military machine? Well, there was always plenty of time for
America to push ahead.

The Kennedy administration was correct that there was no
missile gap. Eisenhower had left Kennedy great strategic and
conventional military strength. In 1962, Russian freighters proved
to be no match for American naval might, and the threat of a
nuclear war that the Russians would lose made Nikita Khrushchev blink.

But Kennedy and McNamara erred in their hope that the
Soviets would follow America's example and restrain themselves.
The policy of unilateral restraint assumed, among other things,
the existence of an American intelligence capability that would
keep us apprised of Soviet actions. In fact, our intelligence mis-
calculated badly. Within a few short years, Pentagon experts were
claiming that the Soviets had caught up.

Startled by this information, Kennedy's successor, Lyndon Johnson, tried to get the Soviets to sit down and talk about stopping the arms race. American policy was to pursue a strategic arms limitation treaty (SALT).

This was an undeniable shift in the liberal Democrats' policy. Only a few years before, they had self-righteously promised to overcome the "missile gap" to keep America first. Now they were calling for "parity," hoping to strike a bargain that would keep the Russians from running away with the arms race altogether. Let's stop this nonsense, they argued. The cost of developing new weapons is a drain on our economies. Let's call the arms race a draw and stay right where we are.

The push for a treaty with the Russians was further popularized by the theory of mutual assured destruction (MAD). It really didn't matter how many missiles the Russians had, liberals said, as long as we had enough to destroy them. What difference did another three hundred missiles make, one way or the other? A nuclear war would mean the end of the world anyway. We had our deterrents. Even if American missiles were outnumbered, liberals argued, they were most certainly more accurate than their Soviet counterparts. Now was the time to strike a bargain.

This shift in liberal strategy was prompted by disillusionment over the growing costs of government social programs and over the ever-escalating Vietnam War. Furthermore, America was entering a period of self-examination and self-criticism. Liberals were becoming ashamed of America's role in Vietnam. Many of them weren't so sure that American nuclear superiority was a good thing.

We conservatives were deeply troubled. A liberal administration had let America fall far behind. Nevertheless, most of us reluctantly supported a bipartisan nuclear treaty of some kind. Faced with a Vietnam War–weary Congress, SALT seemed to be the only option. Of course, we conservatives had our reservations. First, such a treaty should not lock America into an inferior position that could tempt the Soviets to try nuclear blackmail.

Second, such a treaty should include an accurate system of verification.

A LIBERAL LOOK AT THE
SOVIET UNION

What worried conservatives even more than the treaty we would get was the new rationale that liberals were using to get us to the negotiating table. The liberal view suggested that the United States and the Soviet Union had much more in common than we had ever realized. Americans were told that we were just as ignorant of the Russian people as they were of us. If we could somehow look beyond the Cold War propaganda of the 1950s, they told us, we would see people like ourselves, very much afraid of war. The liberals were suggesting that the Soviets could be trusted.

The fact that Russia was so anxious to build such a massive nuclear advantage could easily be explained by her troubled history, liberals told us. She had fought wars on her borders for centuries. There were battles with the Japanese, the Chinese, the Finns, the Turks, the Iranians, the Poles and, several times, the Germans. Much of her extraordinary border had been contested at some time or another. In World War II, she had paid a bloody price. Some estimates suggested that 30 million civilians and soldiers had died, almost ten percent of her population.

No wonder she was paranoid, liberals argued. No wonder she feared an armed America! It was not that she was aggressive. Her threats were only bluff, much like our own political rhetoric in election campaigns. As for their pledges to worldwide revolution and toppling governments, and manifestos blatantly calling for mass murder—well, the Russians abandoned pure Leninism long ago. Most Soviet leaders were quite pragmatic and didn't take such fiery revolutionary talk literally. The Soviet Union was like an old colonial empire now, we were told. It had its hands full with all its satellites and colonies.

And what was the purpose of these liberal arguments? Why was it so important for them to portray Russia as still traumatized by the horrors of World War II, suffering under the load of a failing economy, suspicious of the devotion of its allies and paranoid about a powerful American culture that it couldn't understand?

Why did liberals want us to believe that Russia was really apolitical and no longer believed what Marxism taught about the insignificance of a million or even two million lives lost to advance the worldwide revolution? Why did liberals insist on ignoring what the Soviets themselves said about their intentions?

It was because of a fervent desire for peace, sincere and apparently strong enough to blind liberals to the danger and the reality. They saw Russian leaders as reasonable because they wished them to be. This phenomenon has not been uncommon in history, bearing a chilling resemblance to Chamberlain's appeasement of Hitler in 1938.

But if the liberals were right, if the Russian leaders were reasonable folk just like us, then there was little danger in dealing with them as we conservatives saw them, a sinister and cruel enemy. Their reasonableness would come through as we negotiated and strove for disarmament.

If, on the other hand, the liberals were wrong, if the Russian leadership were what it said it was, dedicated to Marxist-Leninism, a dangerous doctrine justifying any means to its self-righteous end, then we were in serious trouble if we thought of them as "just like us." It was a dangerous time for the free world.

FACING THE REALITIES
OF THE SOVIET EMPIRE

CHAPTER

12

Liberal revisionist historians to the contrary, the Vietnam War was never a conservative war. It was launched and reached its peak during two very liberal Democratic administrations. It was wound down and eventually ended during a moderate Republican administration.

In October of 1961, President Kennedy dispatched his principal military adviser, General Maxwell Taylor, to South Vietnam. Taylor was to assess the threat that insurgent Communists posed and to determine to what extent they might be sponsored by their powerful Communist neighbors to the north. Following Taylor's visit, the United States government began to increase its aid to South Vietnam. Within a year, Kennedy had sent more than fifteen thousand "advisers" to help prop up the Saigon government. In his 1963 State of the Union address, President Kennedy pronounced that "the spear point of aggression has been blunted in South Vietnam."[1] Defense Secretary Robert McNamara predicted that the United States military role would end by 1965.[2]

By the summer of 1963, Kennedy's policymakers became convinced that the South Vietnam government itself was the biggest obstacle to resolving the conflict. They condemned the regime of Ngo Dinh Diem as "despotic and cruel." Many Americans shared this evaluation. Public opinion was particularly incensed by Diem's wife, Madame Nhu, and her religious war against the Buddhists. Under Secretary of State George Ball worried that Diem and his wife "were destroying what little justification we had for being in Vietnam."[3]

Throughout the summer and early fall, numerous telegrams and secret government memos, not only at the Defense Department and the Central Intelligence Agency, but also at the State Department and the White House itself, suggested that the Saigon government had to go. When Kennedy finally made his decision to withdraw support from Diem, South Vietnamese generals and their armies seized government buildings, radio stations and key airports. Though Madame Nhu escaped, Diem and his brother were brutally murdered.

In spite of the revelations of the Pentagon Papers, much of what happened in those months still remains top secret. Other pertinent documents and even tape-recorded White House conversations are sealed at the Kennedy Library, where they will be shielded from curious scholars and public examination for many years to come. To what extent, if any, the American government and its young president were involved in the assassination of Diem and his brother will probably not be determined for some time. What we do know, with hindsight, is that in 1963, a young, liberal administration led us into a very messy political and military situation.

Liberal revisionists would later say that the Vietnam War was not an authentic part of Kennedy's legacy. Some even suggested that he had plans to end it. Most would fiercely contend that had he lived, it would never have advanced much further. But history suggests that the opposite is true.

Kennedy's successor, President Lyndon Johnson, kept the team intact. Not only did he retain Kennedy's cabinet, he even kept the slain president's key advisers. Johnson carried the liberal domestic agenda to heights never dreamed, and the war in Vietnam as well, committing more than a half-million American soldiers. The slain president's brother, Robert F. Kennedy, would support the war three years after his brother's death.

It is true that we few modern conservatives in the early 1960s did join liberals in supporting America's role in Vietnam. We believed their reasons for coming to the defense of Southeast Asia were right. Later, we would join the chorus calling for American withdrawal, though for reasons critically different from the liberals' reasons. But Vietnam was not our show. It was staged at the very height of the liberals' powers. *They* determined its limits and conducted it, and they eventually grew sick of the mess and developed the naive and radical rationale for quitting that is still at the very heart of their philosophy of foreign affairs.

THE WATCHMAN ON THE WALLS

America's entry into the Vietnam War was predicated upon two assumptions. First, that the fall of South Vietnam would inevitably result in a Communist takeover of all of Southeast Asia and thus threaten the security of the United States itself. This so-called domino theory, which would later come under liberal fire and ridicule, was very much a part of liberal foreign policy in the mid-1960s. In July of 1963, in his last public remarks on the Vietnam War, Kennedy told members of the press that "we are not going to withdraw from that effort. In my opinion, for us to withdraw from that effort would mean a collapse, not only of South Vietnam, but Southeast Asia. So we are going to stay there."[4]

Second, it was assumed that the collapse of South Vietnam would result in the deaths of thousands, perhaps millions, of people. Such was the pattern of Communist takeovers. As leader of the free world and champion of world freedom and liberty, America was thought to have a responsibility to use its great power to defend helpless nations from Communist expansion. To that end, in September of 1954, the United States had committed itself to the Southeast Asia Treaty Organization. Third World nations facing insurgencies funded and directed by foreign Communist superpowers would not have to face them alone.

Among the last words penned by liberal President John Kennedy was the speech he was to deliver in Dallas that fateful day, November 22, 1963. Kennedy planned to discuss the "painful, risky, and costly effort in Southeast Asia," warning that "we dare not weary of the task . . . our mission in the world is to carry the message of truth and freedom to all the far corners of the earth. We in this country are, by destiny rather than choice, the watchmen on the walls of world freedom."[5]

Within two years, Americans grew tired of the watch, and many liberals began redefining America's role in the world. Antiwar demonstrations began to sweep American campuses and streets.

Many people attributed the disillusionment to an efficient media that, for the first time, brought home, with terrible vividness and realism, the horrors of war. Others credited the frustration to the false promises of a quick resolution to the Vietnam conflict. The optimistic "light at the end of the tunnel" predictions are now popularly attributed only to the Pentagon but, in fact, throughout the 1960s, they had been coming from the White House and State Department as well.

By the 1968 presidential elections, the American people—Democrat and Republican, liberals and the new emerging modern conservatives—had decided that we must withdraw from Vietnam. Tumbling dominoes notwithstanding, America could not endure much longer the terrible division that racked her society.

Whatever small gains were made on the battlefield in Southeast Asia were more than lost in the court of world opinion, where communism was waging its great battles. Anti-Americanism was spreading worldwide, threatening to create Soviet allies out of otherwise neutral and friendly regimes, allowing Marxist nations to seize leadership in the Third World and even straining America's relationships with her most trusted allies.

In 1968, it was no longer possible to argue that the loss of South Vietnam posed a direct threat to the security of the United States. Indeed, most agreed, regardless of their political philosophy, that under the self-imposed limitations she had placed on her execution of the war, America must get out quickly. The war itself, even if it were successful, posed the greater threat.

But the reason that had first prompted American involvement in Vietnam also delayed her departure. We had made promises. We had championed the hopes of free people all over the world. We said that we would stand by them in the face of foreign Communist aggression. Did we not have a responsibility for the hundreds of thousands, or even millions, who would be slaughtered in a Communist takeover? Americans were stuck in a dilemma.

President Nixon was elected in 1968 on the promise of "peace with dignity." Nixon's concept of transferring the war to South Vietnamese shoulders was at once simple and brilliant. The president never deviated from his gradual but consistent withdrawal of American soldiers, thus gaining enough public support to neutralize the proliferating media and antiwar opposition. Nixon was able to check the worldwide Marxist propaganda victories with apparent concessions and reasonableness in the face of North Vietnamese intransigence. And, finally, the plan gave America time to explore other strategic opportunities for bringing a balance of power to Southeast Asia.

In this latter gambit Nixon has been proven by history to be most skillful. Not all of the dominoes that America was willing to let fall, fell after all. However, it has not been moral restraint that has kept Vietnam from invading Thailand, or from coming to the aid of Communist insurgents in Malaysia and seizing the strategic Straits of Malacca and forming one more knot in the noose around the neck of the Western world. If Vietnam had developed a conscience, she could hardly have been so cruel in starving her conquered comrades in Cambodia. Certainly, it is not out of any fear of America that she has held back.

What has brought a balance of power to Southeast Asia and kept Vietnam from further adventurism has been its "punishing" war with the People's Republic of China, which cannot afford to see a Soviet-backed Vietnam gobble up Southeast Asia. So the dominoes have, for the moment, stopped falling.

But for Watergate, Nixon's carefully worked entree with the People's Republic of China might eventually have helped South Vietnam the way it now serves the sovereignty of other nations in Southeast Asia. In any event, the advent of a Sino-American relationship aided the Nixon plan of a phased withdrawal of support from Vietnam without, at the same time, abrogating our moral responsibility.

THE NEW ANTI-AMERICANISM

With the election of Richard Nixon, the most radical liberals began calling for the unconditional and unilateral withdrawal of all American forces from Vietnam. The process should not be delayed, they insisted. But what about Kennedy's idea of America as the "watchman on the walls of world freedom"?

The answer to that, radical liberals now believed, was that America had no responsibility whatsoever to a regime as corrupt as the one in South Vietnam. Indeed, a growing number of the radical liberals saw a nobility and an integrity in the North Vietnamese government that they couldn't see in our own. These radical leaders declared flatly that America was morally bankrupt. So how could we champion our way of life to others?

Yes, we were told, the Marxist totalitarian states have political prisoners, but so does the United States. They claimed there were thousands languishing in prisons right here. What was Angela Davis, if not a political prisoner?

In retrospect, it seems absurd that radical liberals could compare the few American revolutionaries and terrorists of the 1960s with the millions of political prisoners in Siberian camps and archipelagos. America's revolutionaries of the 1960s were not innocent dissidents; they were professionals who knew how to make Molotov cocktails, planted bombs, issued death threats and, in one case, wired a shotgun to the head of the judge who was to consider their case and dragged him from his courtroom.

Those millions of political prisoners in the Soviet Union or the People's Republic of China, by contrast, were not terrorists or gunmen or anarchists. Their crimes were something they said, or some innocent thing they did, such as requesting the right to emigrate or even to travel abroad. Some were in prison for "exhibiting capitalistic tendencies"—violating some silly technicality, such as overproducing in an assembly line, which a supervisor marked down as "selfish and egotistical individualism at the expense of the collective."

How could the prosecution and sentencing of American terrorists—who had violated the law, kidnapped, blown up buildings, killed innocent people, extorted money or robbed banks—be compared with the torture of Nobel Prize winners in prison cells? How could our system of criminal justice be compared with that of the KGB and the GRU, which compromised science and medicine by experimenting with drugs on their own citizens?

But those radical liberals separating themselves from other liberal Americans insisted that we were no better than our Soviet or Chinese rivals. Marxist totalitarian governments sometimes sentenced prisoners without trials, but blacks in the Old South had suffered the same fate. Some liberals admitted that millions died under Mao Zedong, Lenin and Stalin, but the Soviets themselves had denounced those mass murders. Besides, America practiced genocide on the American Indians. Entire tribes were wiped out. Read the story of the Cherokee Trail of Tears, they would tell us. And what about the more recent atrocities at My Lai? The West was in decline, growing corrupt and arrogant, they warned, even as communism was becoming more pragmatic and less provincial.

These outspoken liberals compared the Soviet invasions of Hungary in 1956 and Czechoslovakia in 1968 with Lyndon Johnson's invasion of Santo Domingo when its government seemed unsuitable to him. They have their satellites and zones of influence, we were told, and we have ours.

The difference was that the freely elected Santo Domingan government had been destabilized by nationals trained in Cuba and equipped with Soviet weapons. Although the Marxist revolutionary army on the island numbered less than two thousand men, it threatened, with Cuban advice and direction, to exploit the civil war between moderates and conservatives. The Marxists were outnumbered, but not when the power of Cuba was added.

If Fidel Castro had been allowed to choose his own satellites in the Caribbean, the whole region would have been threatened. Other governments would have toppled, not by popular revolutionary majorities, but by political machinations heavily financed and directed by Cuba and the Soviet Union and assisted at key moments by assassination squads.

Finally, it was concern for American lives that prompted Lyndon Johnson's action. Armed Marxist guerrillas in Santo Domingo had burst into downtown hotels, looking for opportunities to "shoot Americans."[6] President Johnson's invasion saved thousands of innocent lives from unnecessary bloodshed. A few months later, American forces were withdrawn to allow the people of Santo Domingo to choose their own government.

The Soviet Union, on the other hand, did not invade Hungary or Czechoslovakia to protect Soviet citizens, nor did it invade in order to check the progress of American or Western-trained guerrillas attempting to overthrow the governments of those countries. In both cases, the Soviets simply objected to Communist governments that refused to submit to their wishes. Soviet tanks and armored divisions remain in both countries to this day.

Likewise, it was a gross misrepresentation for liberals to argue that American "zones of influence were no different" from the captive nations of the Soviet Union. Our military defended Japan. We protected her sea-lanes for the oil she imported. We provided defense against her powerful Sino-Soviet–North Korean neighbors. Yet, in spite of all this, Japan didn't hesitate to impose hefty quotas on American automobiles, shoes and goods, even as she exported her own products by the millions to us. Our allies were much different from Soviet captive nations. Our allies had the confidence of much-loved brothers, unthreatened and sure of their position.

Soviet captive nations, meanwhile, saw their industries and natural resources exploited, their armies used as proxies for Marxist wars in far-off continents, their secret services used to assassinate foreign leaders when the Soviets wanted to avoid repercussions. When they attempted their own limited foreign-policy initiatives, they were usually canceled at the whim of the Kremlin.

The most troubling comparison radical liberals offered between American and its Marxist rivals was the equation of Soviet-inspired assassinations with alleged American plots to "terminate with extreme prejudice." There was the circumstantial evidence pointing to American participation in the "termination" of Ngo Dinh Diem, for example, and the controversy surrounding the assassination of Salvador Allende in Chile.

But this was like comparing the terrible criminal violence of a handful of American soldiers at My Lai with the systematic genocide of the Cambodian people under Pol Pot. Not only was there a very substantial difference in degree, but under the American system there were investigations, congressional inquiries, trials and accountability.

In 1984, a CIA-published manual discovered in Central America prompted a storm of outrage and a promise by a conservative president to fire whoever was responsible. The offending pages of the manual included instructions to freedom fighters on how to assassinate key leaders of a target country. That same month, the publication of *Inside Soviet Intelligence,* by former Soviet Intelligence Commander Victor Suvorov, prompted little comment. Suvorov's detailed explanation of the infrastructure of that establishment should have made America pause. One special unit he identified, the Spetsnaz Brigade, included thirteen hundred professional killers. Anxiously awaiting admission to this elite force were another 31,200 members of Soviet military intelligence, trained in assassination.

ROMANTICIZING MAO

The more radical liberals not only insisted that America was just as evil as its Marxist totalitarian counterparts, they even believed that in some circumstances communism was much superior to our own way of life.

Liberals of the 1960s were especially fond of claiming that Marxism had transformed the People's Republic. The fact that Taiwan was three times as rich and that the People's Republic of China had been founded by the mass murder of some 30 million people was casually dismissed with the same ignorance and bigotry that anti-Semites of today display in dismissing the Holocaust as a fabrication. To call the People's Republic of China a success, liberals had to abandon the Judeo-Christian principles that were at the very foundation of Western civilization.

Still, the myth persisted that Marxism in China had created a perfect model for the rest of Asia. The Western media naively accepted the data put out by the People's Republic of China. These facts could not be verified. China was inaccessible. Liberals were taking Mao's own word for China's success.

Years later, America's liberal community reluctantly had to change its tune. When the doors eventually opened and Western journalists visited China, the myth was shattered. *Time* magazine would eventually refer to "an economy laid waste by twenty years of Maoist experimentation." China's new leader, Deng Xiaoping, would institute reforms amounting to what some historians would call "the capitalization of China."[7]

Nevertheless, in the 1960s, the liberal argument prevailed, for Americans wanted to believe it. If Marxism was okay, maybe even superior to capitalism in some regions of the world, then withdrawal from Southeast Asia really wouldn't hurt anybody.

The small but emerging modern conservative movement warned that our tactical decision to withdraw should not panic us into drawing wrong conclusions about our role in the world. But nobody was really listening. So unpopular was the Vietnam War that any attempt to debate its morality was upstaged by the political reality that we had to get out.

A RADICAL DEMOCRATIC PARTY

Increasingly, the radical perception of America plotting the assassination of foreign leaders, jailing political dissidents and imposing its will on other nations began to dominate the liberal movement and the Democratic party. When George McGovern campaigned for president in 1972, he charged that the Nixon administration was the most corrupt government in American history.

All of this was embarrassing for some Democratic politicians who insisted that they were just as patriotic as anybody else. They wanted to get out of Vietnam because it was "a war we couldn't win," or, perhaps more important, because the cost in human lives had become intolerable. Some insisted that assurances of South Vietnam's ability to fend for herself were desirable, if improbable. They called for a rather idealistic negotiated settlement that would have all factions represented in a new South Vietnamese coalition. But the Democratic party had become so radicalized that such proposals began to sound moderate or even conservative. The press began to identify some Democrats as "liberal on domestic policy, but conservative on foreign."

It is important to point out that the anti-Americanism of the 1960s paralleled the transition that was taking place in liberal thought regarding government's role in providing social services and combating crime. Liberals charged that American society and its political system were flawed. Welfare recipients were not getting "welfare" at all, they were getting "entitlements" as compensation for the discrimination or injustice the American system had "perpetrated" against the poor, the minorities, the elderly. Likewise, it was the American system that was to blame for crime. One would have thought that the criminal was the victim.

These beliefs were consistent with the new liberal foreign policy, which suggested that America's "exploitation" of other lands made her an unfit protector of anybody else's interests. Liberals called for America to withdraw as the "world's policeman" and get her own house in order.

When America's withdrawal from Vietnam did come, liberals claimed a great ideological victory. Since they had been the first to call for withdrawal, the fact that the rest of America, including conservatives, eventually agreed was to them a tacit endorsement of their beliefs. It was not just an admission of diplomatic and military error, they claimed, but an admission that the American system and its government were morally wrong.

THE WORLD POLITICS
OF NAIVETÉ

Today, there is a new, more sophisticated version of this argument. Liberal Democrats are careful to wave the flag vigorously at party conventions, yet when the occasion arises, they still ask the same questions. "What is the difference between America's invasion of Grenada and the Russian invasion of Afghanistan?" they will ask, implying that America is just as imperialistic as the Soviet Union.

In fact, America's invasion of Grenada highlights the contrast between liberal and conservative concepts of international responsibility. The Marxist prime minister of that island country had visited Washington shortly before the invasion. He warned that Cuban and Soviet involvement there was threatening the national sovereignty of his people. He explained that a Soviet/Cuban-sponsored jet runway, fully capable of handling Russian MIG-21's, was under construction. Still, when presented with the rather awkward request that the United States send in troops to help a Communist regime resist takeover by its own allies, President Reagan cautiously declined to become involved.

The Prime Minister of Grenada returned to his island where he was murdered weeks later. A Cuban-backed regime promptly took power, and more than a thousand American students studying on the island became potential hostages. When Cuban soldiers herded them into quarantine, another dangerous and disgraceful situation, reminiscent of the Iran crisis, was fully possible. President Reagan's decision to invade Grenada in 1983 was quite similar to President Johnson's decision to invade Santo Domingo in 1965. Besides liberating thirteen hundred Americans, it served once more to check Cuban violations of the sovereignty of Western hemisphere nations.

The contrast to Russia's invasion of Afghanistan could not have been greater. There were no American troops in Afghanistan, no advisers building a runway big enough to accommodate our Phantom F-14's. Nor had we murdered the head of state.

At first, liberals registered great outrage over the Grenadan invasion. Counting on the Vietnam syndrome, some liberals evidently expected an outpouring of demonstrations. But polls showed the American people overwhelmingly supported the action. The rescued students praised President Reagan, and a liberal Democrat running for president backed down from his initial criticism, eventually supporting the administration.

It was not out of ignorance that Americans backed their government while, at the same time, understanding the sinister and aggressive implications of Soviet actions. Americans simply would not agree that our government had imperialistic designs, nor were they convinced that the Soviet Union was like any other nation, except for its historical paranoia about its borders. There were real differences between the West and the Marxist totalitarian states, and no amount of liberal rhetoric could persuade Americans otherwise.

It is curious that after all these years, with the bitterness of the Vietnam War far behind us, liberals are still trying to fan the fires of national self-criticism. They wonder, if we distrust the Russians and regard them as evil because of what they do, what must the Soviets think of us when we do similar things? Perhaps our conflict is all a misunderstanding. The Soviets think we are evil and we think they are evil, when, in fact, we are both frightened nations, stuck together on this little planet. With a little bit of patience, liberals theorize, we might be able to resolve our problems.

It is a different version of the same old argument. And it serves a different purpose. In the 1960s, liberals argued that we weren't any better than the Russians, so what right did we have to be an arbitrator among nations? In the 1980s, liberals argue that the Russians aren't any worse than we are. Therefore, with a little patience, we could build a relationship based on mutual trust.

This explains why President Jimmy Carter was so publicly surprised and hurt by the Russian invasion of Afghanistan. "They broke their word," he said. This even brought a laugh from the liberal press, which occasionally ridicules even the political leader of the very ideology to which most of them subscribe. Of course, many other Americans were disturbed by what they felt to be the President's naiveté. Jimmy Carter was a very sincere and decent man, but the world of reality and the world of liberal fantasies were not the same place.

A CONSERVATIVE PERSPECTIVE

Not everybody had been caught up in the fashionable anti-Americanism and self-criticism of the Vietnam period. There were moderates and liberals who had become quite defensive about the radical position. There were many ordinary Americans, nonpolitical workers and farmers and senior citizens not involved in the rancorous ideological debate, who were troubled by the national self-criticism swirling around them. Some surveys and politicians speculated that they constituted a "silent majority," adding to the emerging conservative movement.

It was their silence, of course, that allowed liberals to have such an impact on American foreign policy. The emerging modern conservatives were the only part of this new alliance that seemed to have a voice. Liberals like to protest that conservatives don't have "a corner on patriotism." But the fact remains that modern conservatives were practically the only people in the 1960s still publicly defending the morality of the American system. We declared that our opposition to Marxist totalitarian expansionism was fully justified. History would hold us accountable, we contended, if we did nothing to stop the certain bloodbath that followed Communist revolutionary takeovers.

Conservatives pointed to the irony that Americans fascinated with Marxist theories could promote their views, while the very American government they savaged protected their right to dissent. They enjoyed a privilege that Vietnam, North Korea and the Soviet Union would not allow their people. While Western intellectual romantics embraced Marxism, thousands, even millions, of people fled totalitarian regimes for the West.

The first little peep out of the so-called silent majority came in the late 1960s when bumper stickers appeared across the heartland of the country with a simple message: "America—Love It or Leave It." If life in Russia or the People's Republic of China or Cuba were truly great, if America were truly hypocritical and evil, then why not go?

Of course, the liberals' answer was fair enough. "This is our country too," they said. "It belongs as much to us as to anybody else. Why should we leave?" And conservatives understand that it's not a very easy thing to walk away from one's own country.

Yet, conservatives pointed out, those refugees of Marxist totalitarian states were doing exactly that, fleeing by the millions for years. Their governments had mined rivers, built walls, patrolled borders and ordered soldiers to shoot to kill. Still, the flood had not been stemmed. In 1956, Hungarians crossed the crowded bridge of Andau by the tens of thousands in only a few short days. Factory workers, side by side with college professors and medical doctors, carried everything they owned in bundles on their backs.

After the Vietnam War, even with the Marxist propaganda gains and with more sophisticated and less public methods of repression, the pattern was the same. While liberals in the Carter administration were trying to suggest that the Sandinistan government was not really Leninist, sixty-two thousand refugees were fleeing Nicaragua into Honduras. In 1982, after reporting massacres at the hands of the Sandinistans, thirteen thousand Mesquito Indians fled Nicaragua. Four million Afghans left after the Soviet invasion in 1980. In 1983, another hundred thousand Cubans left their island. Forty-six thousand East Germans emigrated to the West, and twenty-six thousand emigrated legally from the People's Republic of China into Hong Kong, while ten times as many fled across the borders without permission. One hundred thousand Poles fled after martial law was declared in 1981, pushing their total to more than 1.2 million emigrated since 1975.

The total refugees from Marxist totalitarian states, in our generation alone, numbers at least 25 million, and may, according to some estimates, exceed 50 million. If formed into one nation, they would constitute a mighty cultural, diplomatic and, quite possibly, military power. It would include some of the world's finest dancers and musicians, athletes and Nobel Prize winners. It would include the most brilliant scientists. And it would place well in the top five nations in any Olympic competition. It is not surprising that a disproportionate number of these refugees are the most talented people of their respective nations. For it is easier for the elite to escape a Marxist society than it is for the average peasant on a collective farm.

This flight of millions of refugees, twentieth-century pilgrims who landed on the shores of America and its allies, spoke most eloquently against Marxism and what it could do to people. When the Vietnam War finally ended and the bloodbath in Southeast Asia began, many Americans remembered the sneers and ridicule with which liberal commentators had dismissed such a possibility. But the slaughter in Southeast Asia was not a fantasy of American "bleeding heart" conservatives, it was a savage reality. When the story eventually broke, it was kept buried in the back pages of the liberal press. As many Americans watched and read, they drew their own conclusions about what was happening in the dangerous and painful world around them. America was not flawed; rather it was American liberalism that was flawed. Liberalism had succumbed to the very danger it had always warned would come to the political Right. It had been captured by the voices of extremism. Its threat was not only its distorted view of the world, but its power over the American Establishment.

THE DIFFERENCE

In 1983, in a public address, President Reagan referred to the Soviet Union as "an evil empire." This characterization brought a howl of protest from liberals who said it wasn't true, and from moderates who argued that even if it were true, it was too dangerous to state publicly. But conservatives warned that the Soviet Union and other totalitarian Marxist states have a different agenda from our own. Their methods are different. Their purposes are different, because, most important of all, their philosophy of life and government is different. The American system sprang from a Judeo-Christian culture. Communism, on the other hand, was defined by Karl Marx as "militant materialism," or "militant atheism," or "naturalized humanism."[8]

When Lenin later defined it, he declared flatly, "Marxism is materialism. As such, it is as relentlessly hostile to religion as was the materialism of the Encyclopediasts of the 18th century or the materialism of Feuerbach. This is beyond doubt."[9]

Lenin was often asked to explain the ethics of Marxism. What kind of morality allowed for the creation of a new class in order to create a classless society? How could revolutionaries exploit people in order to end exploitation? How could they lie, censor and seize printing presses in the name of truth?

"In what sense do we reject morality?" Lenin answered.

In the sense given to it by the bourgeoisie who based ethics on God's commandments. On this point, we, of course, say that we do not believe in God and that we know perfectly well that the clergy, the landowners, and the bourgeoisie invoke the name of God so as to further their own interests as exploiters.

We say that our morality is entirely subordinated to the interests of the proletariat's class struggle. Our morality stems from the interests of the class struggle of the proletariat. The old society was based on the oppression of all the workers and peasants by the landowners and capitalists. We had to destroy all that and overthrow them, but to do that, we had to create unity. That is something that God cannot create.[10]

As the Russian Communist leaders continue their unrelenting quest throughout the world, they encourage violence, deception and whatever tactics are needed to secure their ends, because to them the end justifies the means.

We conservatives admit that there may be parallels between what liberal America does and what Russia does. There are parallels between the "militant atheism" of Marx and Lenin and the liberal-secularism of modern America. And "militant materialism" may have its parallel in conservative political philosophy that portrays the entrepreneur as the ultimate hero and too willingly applauds any success and suspects any failure. Both militant atheism and materialism hold up man, not God, as the center of all things, and thus reduce morality to whatever is right or wrong for human purposes and pleasures. But, as Solzhenitsyn points out, "If, as claimed by humanism, man were born only to be happy, he would not be born to die."

Similarities between Marxist totalitarian states and the West? Yes. But that does not mean the two are the same. There are great distinctions. For example, the issues of personal and state morality are still argued in the West. Criminal behavior, whether by a citizen or president or prime minister, is the subject of great public debate and interrogation by a free press. There is free judicial and legislative inquiry.

There can be no doubt that the political battle in America has moved increasingly away from our founding principles. Whereas we once debated whether a policy was right or wrong, we have now begun to debate whether right and wrong even exist as absolutes, or whether they are only a means to a mutually agreed-upon end. But at least there is debate in the West. On the other side of the Berlin Wall, beyond the tank traps and barbed wire and towers with guards carrying guns and binoculars, there are only darkness and silence.

It is ironic and yet very instructive to note that the argument in the West has moved so far to the Left that the modern conservative American can find no more eloquent description of the duty assigned to him than the words that a young liberal president, assassinated by a Marxist fanatic, never had a chance to say. "Our mission in the world is to carry the message of truth and freedom to all the far corners of the earth. We in this country are—by destiny rather than choice—the watchmen on the walls of world freedom."

AN AMERICAN
STRATEGIC FOREIGN
POLICY

CHAPTER

13

If America is once again to assume her role as the champion of spiritual freedom and individual liberty in the world, she must first deal with the very serious threat posed by the Soviet Union. It is no longer a question of whether or not we will enforce the Monroe Doctrine in the Western hemisphere, or revive the Southeast Asia Treaty Organization, or reassert the Truman Doctrine in the Middle East. Those historical commitments, which typified the moral and military self-confidence of our first 175 years, have been abandoned.

America cannot be counted on to champion the freedom of anyone else effectively until she reaffirms that her own freedom is worth defending. But time is running out.

Ironically, having spent her conventional military might in the Vietnam War, she is left with only a nuclear deterrent as her defense—hardly a deterrent at all if administered with self-doubt. If the Russians invaded Western Europe or seized the oil fields of the Middle East or threatened our supply of strategic minerals in South Africa, would we really rain atomic bombs upon their heads? That is the tenuous and shaky premise behind our present efforts to hold the mighty Soviet empire at bay.

Would America, which could not endure the sacrifices of a conventional war against a greatly inferior foe, purposefully launch a nuclear war against a superior one? And all for the sake of Western Europe or the Middle East or even, least likely of all, Africa? Yet the loss of any one of these three strategically critical regions would be like forfeiting our queen in a game of chess with a Russian grand master. For all practical purposes, the game would be over.

No one, not even an American president himself, knows for sure at what point nuclear weapons would be our only option, and whether he would have the will to employ them. Ironically, America's self-doubt about her own willingness to defend her way of life may force her to unnecessarily make such a decision. If a Soviet premier ever got it into his head that an American president would not, the temptation to behave aggressively might be too great to resist.

During the Reagan administration, we have learned that a restored American spirit and resolve cannot, in themselves, guarantee safety. America must have the arsenal and capability to resist diplomatic blackmail. We must not only satisfy ourselves that we are strong enough to deter a Soviet nuclear first strike. We must also be strong enough to convince the Soviets of our capability. The great danger of the 1980s has been that the Soviet's relative advantage in both conventional and strategic weapons may tempt her to believe that a war is desirable.

THE AMERICAN MILITARY
DECLINE

President Nixon, who inherited the Vietnam War from Lyndon Johnson, inherited the SALT negotiations as well. Americans were in a mood to accept assurances that the country's nuclear arsenal was sufficient, and they were not about to support the replacement of conventional weapons used up in Vietnam.

The Soviets, meanwhile, continued to ignore the role that Kennedy's and McNamara's unilateral restraint had assigned them. They promptly introduced more powerful and more accurate ICBMs. Nixon eventually convinced a liberal Congress that America must demonstrate some willingness to match the Soviets' arms buildup, or they would have no incentive to negotiate a treaty. By only one vote, the Senate approved the development of a safeguard antiballistic missile system. It was not much, but enough to gain some Soviet concessions. Brezhnev and Nixon met in Moscow to sign SALT I.

President Nixon himself was not satisfied with the treaty. "It allowed the Soviets higher levels than previously deemed acceptable and higher than those permitted the United States, but this simply reflected the realities of the situation at the time, and we intended that the offensive agreement would last no more than five years."[1]

What the treaty did not forbid was the development of the MX missile, the Trident submarine and a new B-1 bomber. Most liberals argued against all three of them. They questioned whether the MX would really be invulnerable to Soviet attack and argued that it would be "absurd in an age of missiles to develop another bomber."[2]

A year after his election, Democratic President Jimmy Carter postponed a decision on the MX missile and canceled the B-1 bomber altogether. In Richard Nixon's *The Real War,* the former president refers to the latter as "one of the greatest strategic blunders this nation has ever made." As a result, the United States's strategic defense continued to rely on a combination of our outdated Minuteman missiles and squadrons of B-52 bombers that were first deployed in the 1950s!

By 1980, Soviet nuclear strategic superiority was an unquestioned fact. We were outnumbered five to one in ICBM's, three to one in total megatonnage, and two to one in numbers of re-entry vehicles. In the following years, the Reagan administration laid the groundwork to catch up, but Soviet productivity was already well in motion.

The American decline in conventional defenses was even more dramatic. By the 1980s, a viable Soviet navy had suddenly appeared. The Russians outnumbered us in both combat vessels (289–173) and attack submarines (257–81). In tanks, they had a six-to-one edge. Their combat-ready army numbered 5 million to our 1 million, and, counting reserves, the difference was staggering. Twenty-five million Russians trained regularly in a reserve army. The United States can call up only an additional two million.

MAD

America's defense during these uncertain years, and indeed, to this day, rests on the rather absurd and appropriately named idea called MAD (Mutual Assured Destruction). Yes, this theory says, the Russians have the capability of destroying us. But we have the capability of destroying them. Stalemate!

MAD becomes an unreasonable theory when the possibility is raised that the United States would resort to mutual destruction over West Berlin, South Korea, Israel or the Saudi oil fields. According to MAD, which was part of the Democrat platform as recently as the 1984 presidential campaign, the United States would be the first to use nuclear weapons in such a situation, since our conventional forces—tanks and armies—would be quite obviously incapable of stopping the Russians. But would we really trigger a terrible nuclear holocaust? If the Russians responded in kind, the world we know would come to an end. So MAD is a policy of suicide, with the whole world as hostage.

It is ironic that in the name of peace, liberals have voted reductions in defense spending, stripping our conventional military capability and leaving us only two options: nuclear war or surrender. Hitler had bacterial and biological weapons but refused to employ them, knowing that his enemies could do the same. Would an American president use an even more terrible nuclear weapon?

Worse still, a growing consensus seems to be that the Soviet Union could win a nuclear war. The Soviet Union has the capability to take out most of our vulnerable Minutemen silos, while leaving our large population centers undisturbed. America would be left with two options. She could launch her missiles from bombers and submarines, which at the present time would probably survive a Russian first strike. But where would we send these missiles? We could direct them at Soviet missiles in silos, but theirs outnumber ours by many times, and, after our bombs had been expended, they would still have the capability of annihilating the rest of the United States. So we would have to target our missiles on Soviet cities. And when we had destroyed Moscow, Leningrad, Kiev, Kharkhov, Gorki and all the other cities, the Russians, with half of their population and all of their missiles still intact, could blow to pieces every little city in America with a population of twenty thousand or more.

There would be another option, of course. After losing our Minutemen missiles in a Soviet first strike, and faced with the specter of the destruction of hundreds of millions of innocent Russian and American civilians, the United States could enter into a negotiated settlement. Participating in an exercise at the request of the president, I was confronted with just such a situation, and this was precisely the course of action recommended to me by State Department officials. The Soviets would probably even let us continue to have elections—supervised, of course. There would be plenty of Americans to teach us about the "superior Soviet system" that we would then be embracing. It would be time for those Americans who have sympathized with the worldwide Marxist revolution to display the bumper stickers, "America—Love It or Leave It." This would be *their* country then.

THE CONSERVATIVE STRATEGY

Conservatives totally reject MAD in the long run. It inevitably limits America to a choice between the possible destruction of our nation by nuclear weapons, and, if Russia determines it is in her best interests, a negotiated settlement with, quite possibly, our eventual destruction by Cambodian-style genocide.

What we have called for is the continued development of strategic weapons until the Soviet Union agrees to stop its own pursuit of nuclear superiority. Conservatives would be quite willing to eliminate all nuclear weapons. But we are not willing to deceive ourselves by a unilateral restraint that only favors the Russians and entices them to end the conflict once and for all.

We conservatives have favored the development of "Star Wars" weaponry: satellites capable of disabling missiles in midair by laser-beam technology. Such a defensive capability would render obsolete all ICBM's. The Russians could then either postpone once more the stabilization and advancement of their troubled economy and launch into another decade of expensive weapons development, or agree with us that the arms race should be halted. There is, of course, no guarantee that Russia would choose the latter, and conservatives contend that America's resolution must be firm and realistic until she does.

Liberals have attacked the whole idea of "Star Wars" weaponry, first on the grounds that it is not technologically feasible. But Americans, who have seen their country land a man on the moon and who love nothing better than a challenge, don't really buy this objection. The crossbow was once a terrible offensive weapon against which there could be no defense. Weapon systems have always alternated between offensive and defensive.

Liberals also say it is a bad precedent to introduce weapons into space. Presumably they mean *our* weapons, for the Soviets have already launched killer satellites. It doesn't matter to liberals that "Star Wars" weapons would be defensive, that they could not "knock out" cities, only the terrible missiles that would otherwise "knock out" our cities. It doesn't matter to liberals that such a system could practically end the threat of ICBM's, and, for the time being, check all fears of a nuclear holocaust. "Star Wars" technology should not be pursued because it violates space, they say. This argument reflects the mysticism of the environmental movement that liberalism has come to embrace. What is in space that liberals would protect? There are no humans there. They would have us believe that it is one thing to build terrible nuclear silos next to someone's farm on earth and quite another thing to invade the darkness and emptiness of outer space.

The most popular liberal argument against a "Star Wars" laser-beam defense is that it would force the Soviets into a first strike. Liberals tell us that the Russians could not tolerate such an effective defense.

But we conservatives believe that America's only hope for neutralizing Soviet strategic and conventional superiority is to employ the only advantage we have left—our technological capabilities. We have an edge—not a great one, but at least an edge. It is our best hope, and we must pursue it, now.

ISRAEL—LINCHPIN OF AN AMERICAN STRATEGIC POLICY

I have often asked college audiences to name the region of the world most vital to America's national security. Invariably, they will say the Middle East, and, of course, they are right. But the reasons are far more complex than they imagine.

"And where," I will ask, "are our American forces stationed?"

"There are twenty thousand in South Korea," they answer, or "We have two hundred thousand in Europe." Some will say, "We have forces in Guam and Japan, and there are several bases in the Philippines and in the Indian Ocean."

"How many American troops are stationed in the Middle East?" I ask, and they look at each other, feeling they have gotten my point before answering back, "None." On the surface, this is a perfectly preposterous situation. The best information available to us suggests that the Soviet Union will need to import oil within ten years or less. A former American president once wrote that never before in the history of the world has so much wealth been so undefended as in the Middle East.

The truth is, however, that the Middle East and her rich oil fields are not undefended at all. Israel and her small, but daring, military machine work to the advantage of both American strategic interests in the region and the interests of the Arab oil nations.

Of course, there is no formal treaty. The Americans and Israelis have not agreed on this end. There are great tactical differences between the two governments—differences that can be so irritating to American presidents and seem so important at the time that they will often complain in their memoirs about the stubbornness of an Israeli prime minister or the unpredictability of his limited foreign policy goals.

Such views of Israel, however, are too narrow to appreciate Israel's grand and critical role in the world balance of power. When we conservatives complain about foreign aid, even aid to Israel, we overlook the fact that if this ally had not existed in the 1970s, the United States herself would have had to intervene in the Middle East, in full strength. We would have been forced to obtain bases and, at the expense of many billions of dollars, maintain a land army with thousands of troops. All this would have been achieved at great diplomatic expense elsewhere.

Let me illustrate by comparing our "aid" to Israel with our "defense" expenditures on behalf of European security. According to a Defense Department report in 1984, "the total cost of European-deployed U.S. forces and all of the U.S.-based forces that we have pledged to contribute as NATO reinforcements amounts to about $177 billion per year."[3] That's sixty-eight times what we spent to assure Middle Eastern security by maintaining the strength of Israel.

And we spend, according to the General Acounting Office,

more on the defense of Europe than the Europeans do. By the GAO's method of comparison, our bill is $106 billion annually, compared with a European bill of $103 billion.[4] Israel, however, spends four dollars on defense for every dollar spent by the United States.

But American liberals are often critical of what they view as Israel's paranoia, her willingness to preempt an invasion by an Arab neighbor with an invasion of her own. The fact is, Israel's unpredictability, her stubbornness, her healthy cynicism born out of a passionate intention never again to submit to genocide, make her the perfect ally to America at a time when our own willpower and commitment to Western values are in question.

It is easy for American liberals to sit back in safety and debate the West Bank settlements or the rights of Palestinians, and to question Israeli policies that they feel may lead to unnecessary bloodshed. But the fact remains, if the Israelis were not there, the United States would have to go in. And no matter how skillfully such a power play were pulled off, if we were invited by the Saudis or the Egyptians or some other government, no amount of diplomatic skill or military efficiency could avoid loss of life and equipment in a protracted American intervention in the dangerous and volatile Middle East. It would be a quagmire much more dangerous than Vietnam, and much more likely to escalate into a superpower confrontation with the Russians.

The commitment of the modern conservative to Israel is both theological and political. Evangelical Christians, for example, take quite literally the scriptural prophecy addressed to Israel, "I will bless those who bless thee and curse those who curse thee." Their commitment is totally unconditional—and timeless.

Politically, conservatives view Israel as an essential ally that has assumed a disproportionate share of the burden to maintain worldwide strategic balance. (This is not an anti-Arab position. It is pro-Mideast. The people of that region of the world can and must live in peace with one another.)

A nice arrangement? Perhaps, for a shortsighted and selfish America. But it is an intolerable one for the Israelis. It is their sons who are dying in a struggle against terrorists and their allies. And Israel doesn't have many sons to give. While America provides a complete defensive umbrella for Japan, allowing her economic prosperity, Israel's economy hovers near the brink of disaster on a month-to-month basis.

It does not matter if Israel and America have been brought together by cultural and political reasons, even without conscious choice. It does not matter that Israel has assumed a role that we have not asked her to assume. All that matters is reality. And today's reality calls for much more responsible American support for Israel.

The extreme commitment of modern conservatives to Israel disturbs many liberals. They do not want to appear less supportive of Israel than we are. Yet liberals and moderates are more apt to talk about the moral rights of Palestinians, the provocation caused by Israeli settlements on the West Bank, the threat to Egypt and Saudi Arabia that a determined pro-Israeli posture would imply. But if conservatives are narrowly committed to the survival of Israel, it is not because they do not appreciate these other concerns. Rather it is because dealing with the Soviet threat in the Mideast is a much higher priority. Israel's strength, with United States support, is at present the only real deterrent to Russian expansion in that vital part of the world.

THE NECESSITY OF AFRICA

As secretary of the interior, I was confronted with the astonishing fact that the United States imports 50 percent of its strategic minerals. Most of these minerals are found in the Soviet Union and in the nations of Africa. It goes without saying that, in a time of increased international tension, the Soviet Union would cut off our supply. The United States could not hope to sustain a protracted nuclear arms race or even a short war without strategic minerals from Africa.

America's relationship with South Africa is especially controversial. While opposing apartheid, the United States has had to maintain access to the sources of its strategic minerals, even when our relationship to South Africa has alienated us from other Third World governments.

Modern American conservatives, whose philosophy has so much to offer blacks in this country, must be careful to define our relationship with South Africa in a way that points to her necessary involvement in checking the Soviet Union without in any way implying endorsement of apartheid.

Some liberals are hypocritical in calling for a break in relations with South Africa even as our relations continue with racist and murderous regimes elsewhere, including the Soviet Union. Even when Idi Amin was murdering thousands in Uganda, chopping off the arms and legs of his victims and forcing prisoners into cannibalism, he was elected president of the Organization of African Unity with hardly a protest from liberals. Black regimes in East Africa have murdered, seized the property of and driven away people of Asian descent who had owned land there for centuries.

It would be catastrophic for America to forfeit her relationship with South Africa in hopes of gaining the sympathy and approval of Third World nations. For no matter what America does, she has already suffered politically for hesitating. Besides, nothing she does will please those Soviet/Cuban–sponsored regimes. Many other African governments already have strong relations with us and a good understanding of America's strategic dilemma. But other regimes, faced with the severe and awesome tasks that plague many Third World countries, are so unstable and have such a high rate of political turnover that virtually nothing America does will guarantee their policies toward us.

Finally, it would be wrong for America to break relations with

South Africa while still maintaining relations with regimes that have waged murderous tribal wars against their own people. Some suggest that by so doing, we would be outmaneuvering the Soviets and Chinese Marxists, going right to the hearts of the people of Africa. In fact, however, much of the diplomatic and propaganda pressure focusing on South Africa, while ignoring the murderous wars that continually rage across the continent, is Soviet-inspired.

The United States must use her diplomatic and economic power to influence South Africa to give dignity and to extend rights to all of its people, regardless of color. We must use our diplomatic skills to carefully explain our complicated dilemma. But we cannot afford simply to abandon South Africa.

Marxists are fond of arguing that time and the worldwide revolution are on their side. Actually the reverse is true. The reputation of Marxist totalitarian states is catching up with them. The bungling and crude attempts of the KGB to manipulate some African governments have left many on the continent disillusioned. In Africa, America can afford to wait, to let the reality of failed Soviet promises and the danger of the Soviet presence soak in.

THE NATO ALLIANCE

Like Israel and South Africa, Western Europe is critical to American defense against the Soviet Union. So powerful are her industrial and technological capabilities, if Russia were to assimilate Western Europe, she could quite easily isolate America within a generation, and probably sooner. With the loss of Western Europe, the world economy as we know it would collapse. In recent years, the Common Market's gross national product has exceeded that of the United States.

There are three ways in which Western Europe is threatened. One is an outright invasion by Soviet and Eastern bloc forces, which greatly outnumber their NATO counterparts. Pentagon theorists hope only that NATO forces could slow down such an invasion to give the Allies sufficient time to airlift troops and mount a proper defense.

Second and equally dangerous would be the political disintegration of NATO. The alliance has already been sorely tested by the independence of the French and the brief ascendancy of a Marxist government in Portugal. Communists have served in the cabinets of Italian and French governments. But even more likely than a disintegration prompted out of sympathy for the Soviet Union would be a disintegration prompted out of fear of the unreliability of the United States as a NATO partner. With each commitment that the United States breaks to governments in Asia, Africa and Latin America, Europe will move closer to an economic and diplomatic accommodation with Russia. There are politicians in every NATO country who subscribe to such a policy. This is how America's stand in El Salvador or South Korea becomes inextricably linked to what happens elsewhere. The balance of power can shift slightly back and forth, but when the tilt becomes too great, huge chunks of support for America will begin to fall off, and suddenly there will be an avalanche.

And, third, Western Europe is quite vulnerable because of its relationship with the Middle East. One of the great dangers of losing Saudi Arabia, for example, is that the loss would precipitate the economic collapse of Western Europe and Japan. So interrelated are the world's economies that even the partial collapse of Western Europe would plunge the world into a terrible and frightening depression. The international banking system would collapse.

The Soviet Union and, to a greater extent, the People's Republic of China, would come through the worldwide crisis only bruised. Both economies, especially that of the Chinese, are less dependent on Western economies. The sparks of revolution, even now alive in Third World countries, could be fanned into flames.

National governments, their tanks stalled for lack of gasoline and oil, their airplanes sitting on runways awaiting spare parts, could not easily resist Soviet-sponsored conventional wars.

THE TERRIBLE REALITY

Such scenarios seem totally unreal to Americans, but the rise and fall of nations and civilizations, the inevitable sufferings of people, are the stuff of history. The pleasures of Versailles may be undisturbed for a generation or two or three. But not forever. The only unchanging fact of history is change itself.

Liberals always sneer at conservative scenarios whose credibility is too often established only after the fact—and sometimes not even then. Conservative warnings of a bloodbath in Southeast Asia were dismissed as silly and emotional. Even when they became fact, they were ignored. Even when the blood of three million innocent civilians soaked Cambodian soil, the whole tragedy seemed too bizarre for some liberals to consider. They did not think it could happen, and therefore, in their minds, it did not.

Reality is much different. Secretary of State Henry Kissinger viewed Saudi Arabia and Iran as the "twin pillars" of stability in the Middle East. This concept was shattered by the Ayatollah's revolution. The Shah was our friend. His military machine was advanced, his economic expansion impressive, his country's strategic position critical. The Shah supplied Israel with 70 percent of her oil. Yet we managed to lose Iran pretty much on our own, even without Soviet assistance.

Who is to say that Saudi Arabia, that other "pillar of stability," where immigrant workers outnumber the nationals three to one, is not vulnerable? And what economist can envision how the oil-based economies of Europe and Japan could survive the collapse of the Middle East?

In Europe, NATO does not spend billions of dollars to maintain its military machine in order to invade the Soviet Union.

Soviet forces outnumber us in equipment and men by many times. But if NATO forces are there for defensive purposes, if we believe that the Soviet Union has the will and desire to do what she has repeatedly said must be done, then how can American liberals suggest, as they have from time to time in recent years, that we bring our troops home? Either there is a threat or there is not a threat.

Of course, it is incredible that modern man, with the power to destroy the world, would still play at war, and still kill other men in the name of humanity, that huge armies would face each other on borders separated by walls and barbed wire. Violence itself is incredible. But it exists. War is still a terrible fact of history. It must be faced and overcome, not out of a hope based on self-deception and ignorance, but out of a hope based on strength and vigilance.

The extermination of the Jews should not be a lesson for Jews only. It should be a lesson for everyone. There are evil people in the world, and there are evil governments. And what they say they will do, no matter how cruel or preposterous it may sound, they may very *well* do. If the West refuses to heed the reports of the 25 million to 50 million pilgrims who have fled Marxist totalitarianism in the last fifty years, then we had better prepare to experience for ourselves a great darkness of the soul—with one added torment. There will be no other world to flee to.

EPILOGUE:
THE COURAGE
OF A
CONSERVATIVE

I numbly got into my chauffeur-driven car to head for another day at the office. It was 7:30 A.M. Fifteen minutes later, I would be seated at my desk making last-minute preparations for the daily 8:00 A.M. meetings. There was always some decision that had to be made. The easy decisions were made in the field or at a lower level. The tough ones came to my desk—relentlessly. Usually I was eager for the next day. I loved making decisions. I had determined that I wouldn't duck any of them. But today was different.

I sat motionless. My chauffeur, Ralph Chinn, was the best. He knew when to talk and when not to say a word. The car was filled with silence.

Could I go on? Did I want to? Was it worth it? The day before, I had testified before a House of Representatives committee. The liberals on the committee weren't interested in facts,

or in establishing an understanding. They wanted headlines and
TV exposure, and they knew they could get both with me. The
Department of the Interior reported to nineteen different House
and Senate committees or subcommittees. Unlike a board of
directors of a corporation, church or charity that wants success
and progress, the majority of the members of almost every committee sought to embarrass, ridicule and demean the Reagan
administration and its spokesmen.

Yesterday had been no exception. My detailed, fact-filled statement was ignored by the members of Congress and censored by
the media. The attack was directed against me personally. That
was how they got headlines. There would be no TV news showing my testimony that all lands under the jurisdiction of the
Department of the Interior were being better managed since the
Reagan administration assumed office. That was a boring fact.
The press wanted an event, personalities in conflict, charges and
denials. The members of Congress knew how to play to the cameras, and the media knew I would not back down under an attack
on my people, programs, personality or religious commitment,
all of which had come under fire at one time or another in the
preceding eighteen months.

Yesterday had been no different from my earlier appearances.
I had refused to yield to an ill-informed liberal member of Congress who was making outlandish charges. I believed that my
people and I deserved to be treated with decency, but decency
doesn't make the evening news, and the liberals knew it. For
eighteen months, I had won on matters of substance while suffering defeat in the battle for a good public image. Was that not
censorship?

As I sat in the car moving down the Rock Creek Parkway, I
reviewed the last year and a half. We had brought a revolution
to the department. We had successfully implemented policies,
regulations, manuals and orders that would last for decades. I was
very proud of our accomplishments. The president's agenda had
been put in place, restoring the parks and wildlife areas, making

energy resources available, and defusing the "Sagebrush Rebellion." My support from the western senators and congressmen had been great. I had told President Reagan that if I were successful in implementing his policies, the political pressure from the Left (special-interest groups and media) would be so great I would no doubt have to be fired after eighteen months. He said he would back me, and he had. But maybe now was the time to go.

Still, we had worked so hard to bring about those changes. Maybe I needed to stay a few more months to ensure them. America couldn't afford to go back to where she had been. In order to carry out the new programs, my people in the Interior Department needed a tough political "street fighter" to take the heat from the press, the special-interest groups and the liberal members of Congress.

But how much more could I take? I was tired way down inside. Several Republican members came up to me after the hearing and commended me for being so tough. A Democrat on the committee called to apologize for the rude treatment his colleagues had given me. But none of these supporters would take a public stand with me in the thick of the battle. In the last several months, calls had come from the White House, the Hill and across the country, urging me not to back down. They were saying, "You have won; don't back off." Reagan supporters across the country wanted a fighter who would bring the revolution the voters had chosen. They were marvelously supportive. But I was so tired.

I picked up my briefcase and stepped out as the car came to a halt. Ralph said, "Have a nice day, sir."

"Thanks, Ralph." The only words spoken.

I stepped into my private elevator to go up to the sixth floor. My mind flashed back to the first time I had been in that small, oak-paneled elevator, built almost fifty years ago. I had been with a tough, self-made man, the governor of Alaska, Wally Hickel. I liked him. He knew what he wanted to do and was determined to do it. In 1969, the Nixon White House gave me the assignment to get Governor Hickel confirmed. I thought it would be easy, but it was not.

The "environmentalists" had come of age and were determined to show their strength. They effectively manipulated two or three United States senators to launch a merciless attack on Hickel. Before the several days of hearings were adjourned, he had agreed to almost all of their liberal demands and was so bruised that he was not the man I had met a few weeks before. He tried to show the liberal environmentalists that he was one of them. Watching him, I learned one could not outrun environmentalists to the political Left. Nixon had to fire Wally after about twenty months.

My mind shifted to 1975 when I was still working in the Department of the Interior and Stan Hathaway, my good friend and former governor of Wyoming for eight years, was named secretary of the interior by President Ford.

We gathered to prepare Stan for the confirmation hearings. He was good. He knew the West. The hearings commenced, and the liberal forces of the environmental movements used willing liberal senators to unleash an ugly attack. The hearings lasted several weeks. The press had a heyday. Truth was irrelevant. It was a ruthless and unscrupulous battle. Stan finally won confirmation, but within a few weeks he resigned with a nervous breakdown that hospitalized him for months.

The same enemies and their philosophical descendants had started attacking me even before my confirmation hearings. They had learned you can beat a man into submission in our political system if you can get the press to do your dirty work. But I had prevailed for eighteen months. I had successfully implemented the president's revolution to restore America's greatness. But maybe my time was up. We knew I couldn't last forever. My job was, for the most part, done.

The elevator doors opened, and I walked to my small working office. Its stark government-issue furnishings and 1930s-vintage, solid oak paneling focused my eyes on the framed Calvin Coolidge quote that I had amended and had printed ten years earlier.

I stood in the middle of the room and, with briefcase in hand, read for the umpteenth time:

Press On:

Nothing in the world can take
the place of persistence.

Talent will not;
Nothing is more common than
unsuccessful men with talent.

Genius will not;
Unrewarded genius is almost
a proverb.

Education will not;
The world is full of educated
derelicts.

Persistence forges results.

I turned to face my roundtable desk and was confronted with the other simple framed item in my office, General Douglas MacArthur's last address to his West Point Academy. Across the top are these large words:

Duty   Honor   Country

I didn't need to read the speech. I knew its spirit. There was no personal sacrifice too great to keep one from doing what one must for America, for out of the rich past of this nation comes the call:

Duty   Honor   Country

Standing in that room all alone, tired and discouraged, I felt those words. I bowed my head and gave a silent prayer to Him from Whom my strength and courage comes.

My discouragement ebbed away, a smile welled up from inside. I was again ready to make decisions in the next round in the battle for America.

The next battle was not long in coming. We conservatives are revolutionaries seeking to bring about change. Change does not come easily. Most people resist change because with it comes uncertainty. People frequently opt for an undesirable status quo rather than deal with the change. Of course, some *like* the status quo. They have an economic position, social status or life-style to defend.

Others who are not as satisfied with their station in life or the state of affairs seek change. But it never comes without conflict, without confronting the old ways, without tension and pressures and hardship and controversy. I know of no one who enjoys controversy, which is often unpleasant, but many will accept it if the objective is worth the cost.

The only thing certain about change is that it is inevitable. We can be overcome by it or absorbed by it, or we can seek to direct it.

Conservatives want to direct it. We believe America can lead the world to a greater quality of life in the twenty-first century. The changes needed for America's greatness to expand are many, and some of them are very severe. But change we must.

We must begin by confronting the failed policies of the past.

1. We conservatives must provide leadership to establish and teach a moral basis for government activity. Our revolution must set free the spiritual nature of our society and withdraw the restraining hand of government so that the strength and wisdom of pluralism is restored.

2. We must lead America in reaffirming the right of individuals to own and enjoy property and in restoring a more open marketplace for the exchange of resources and ideas.

3. We must reduce the size of the federal government and the excessive regulations that limit economic expansion and the creation of jobs.

4. We must reduce federal spending and the tax burden on the individual.

5. We must show our determination to win the struggle against discrimination. Discrimination because of race, sex, color, creed or age is wrong. While we must be tolerant of all people, we must be intolerant of discrimination.

6. We must eliminate subsidies to business and corporate interests.

7. We must provide meaningful assistance to the truly needy, and we must offer them a way back into a productive role in society.

8. We must protect and enhance our natural environment.

9. If America is to assure her own freedom and that of other nations in the twenty-first century, we must lead the way in establishing a true international peace, based on a realistic understanding of ourselves and the world around us.

10. We must aggressively pursue a mutually verifiable total disarmament agreement, but until it is achieved, we must continue to build our conventional and nuclear capability to protect ourselves and the free world.

11. While the liberals may keep their theory of mutual assured destruction, conservatives must lead the American people away from a system based on mutual suicide to a defensive system. We must never lose the hope that since a way was found to release the terrors of the atom, a way must be found to neutralize those terrors as well.

12. We must seek free trade in the world and yet have the self-discipline to deny our markets to countries that do not offer free trade to us.

13. We must be the champions of human rights throughout the world. We must help feed the hungry, not because they are Western or Eastern or Marxist or free, but because they are human beings with dignity.

I have often been asked why I did not finesse the political and philosophical controversies that surrounded my years as secretary of the interior. Couldn't I have done more for the conservative cause and more to restore the greatness of America had I paced myself and been less ideologically visible and outspoken?

My decision to speak out was a conscious and deliberate one. I had served in a variety of top government positions for sixteen years in Washington with little controversy. I had served in our government under five presidents. A man does not find himself a member of his president's cabinet without some political skills. I was very much aware that delivering forthright speeches in the full glare of the liberal media was likely to produce incidents. I knew the personal price.

Some say I could have done more for the modern conservative cause if I had not spoken the truth so loudly and so often. But the liberal Establishment will never be shaken without confrontation. We must be willing to confront it if we want to restore America's greatness.

We need conservatives who will use their political skill and personal discretion to help effect great changes. There are times when we must pace ourselves, or when we should be silent. But there are also times when we must stand and speak up and demonstrate clearly the values that make America.

One of the highlights of every week during my cabinet years was my "Monday Morning Group" meetings. This was a gathering of the forty-five or fifty key political appointees in my department, dedicated to bringing change to America. They were the faithful. They had moved to Washington, changed jobs, abandoned their careers and risked the future to help make a remarkable history that we could look to with pride, as could our children and grandchildren.

This group became family, for we shared both the glory and the ridicule as we moved unrelentingly toward our goals.

One Monday morning, I shared a story with the group. A member of my staff had told me a few days earlier that I reminded him of a scene out of the motion picture, *Bonnie and Clyde,* starring Warren Beatty and Faye Dunaway. "Clyde said to Bonnie, 'Now that they know who I am, things are really gonna get rough. They're gonna come running after me, and anybody else who's with me. Right now, I can't get out. But you still can. So I ain't gonna make you stay, 'cause things are only gonna get worse. If you stay with me, there ain't gonna be a moment's peace.'

"Bonnie smiled, looked into Clyde's eyes and said, 'You promise?'"

"Keep that story in mind," I told my political appointees. "If you stick with me, I guarantee you'll never have a moment's peace."

I was surprised by a thundering ovation from forty-five standing, misty-eyed men and women.

Sometimes when I am asked why I so willingly became a target during my years as a cabinet officer, I remember the marvelous success we had in bringing about the changes needed to restore America's greatness. Sometimes I think of the great honor of standing for and with the president; sometimes I see the faces of those who expressed their gratitude to me for what I was doing; and sometimes I think of the Monday Morning Group, who had the courage to care for a greater America.

After remembering all this, I sometimes answer with a story about General Douglas MacArthur. In his tours of the front line, he was so frequently and needlessly exposed to death that he prompted criticism. A doctor, suggesting that the general's behavior was either suicidal or foolhardy, asked him if he did not realize how important he was to the cause.

The general replied, "If I am brave, my colonels will be. If my colonels are brave, my lieutenants will be. If my lieutenants are brave, my men at the front will be."[1]

There is indeed a battle for America. Time is running out. Those who have the courage to stand and speak out must do so now.

NOTES

Chapter 2. Choosing Sides

1. *Time,* January 21, 1985, p. 55.

Chapter 3. The Liberal Establishment

1. Rothman-Lichter Survey, Research Institute of International Change, Columbia University, New York, 1980.

Chapter 4. The Compassionate Conservative

1. Charles Murray, *Safety Nets and the Truly Needy* (Washington, D.C.: The Heritage Foundation, 1982), p. 3. Charles Murray is perhaps the most eloquent and effective critic of the failed liberal welfare program.
2. *New York Times,* "Relief Is No Solution," February 2, 1962, p. 28.
3. Broadus Mitchell, *Encyclopedia International* (Grolier, Inc., 1963), p. 182.

4. U.S. Bureau of Labor Statistics, *Purchasing Power of the Dollar 1940–1983*, no. 796.

5. Jack Kemp, *An American Renaissance: A Strategy for the 1980s* (New York: Berkley Books, 1981), p. 216.

6. *New York Times*, February 2, 1962, p. 10.

7. Murray, pp. 16–23.

8. Murray, p. 12.

9. Edward I. Koch, *Mayor: An Autobiography* (New York: Warner Books, 1985), p. 137.

10. Koch, p. 137.

Chapter 5. The Betrayal of the American Black

1. "The Murder Epidemic," *Science*, December 1984, pp. 43–48.

2. Patrick Buchanan, "On Black Subsidies to Whites," *Washington Times*, November 28, 1983.

3. Richard Viguerie, "Conservative Alternative Beckons Black Families," *Washington Times*, May 24, 1984, Section C, p. 1.

4. "Black Republicans: What Makes Them Tick?" *Ebony*, August 1984, pp. 72–74.

5. Viguerie, p. 1.

6. Koch, pp. 84, 85.

7. Viguerie, p. 1.

Chapter 6. The Rights of the Victim

1. Victoria Lipnic, "War On Crime: Is the Tide Turning?" *First Monday*, vol. 14, no. 4, 1984, p. 13.

2. The President's Task Force on Victims of Crime, Department of Justice, Washington, D.C., 1982.

3. Thomas Jefferson, "Letter to Justice William Johnson, Monticello, June 12, 1823," in *Jefferson Writings*. Edited by Merrill D. Peterson (New York: The Library of America, Literary Classics of the United States, Inc., 1984), p. 1476.

4. "Polling for Mental Health," *Time*, October 1984, p. 80.

5. Frank Carrington, *Crime and Justice* (Washington, D.C.: The Heritage Foundation, 1983), p. 34.

6. Charles Silberman, *Criminal Violence, Criminal Justice* (New York: Random House, 1978), p. 197.

Chapter 7. A Violent Society

1. George Bush, in remarks made in vice-presidential debate with Geraldine Ferraro, October 11, 1984.
2. "Abortion: The Moral Dilemma, The Medical Issues, The Turn to Violence," *Newsweek*, January 14, 1985, p. 20.
3. "The Hardest Question," *Newsweek*, January 14, 1985, p. 29.
4. C. Everett Koop, M.D., "The Slide to Auschwitz," *Human Life Review*, summer 1982, p. 22.
5. Koop, p. 25.
6. Ibid., pp. 26–27.
7. "TV Violence: The Shocking New Evidence," *Readers' Digest*, January 1983, p. 50.
8. Ibid., p. 50.
9. Ibid., p. 50.
10. Ibid., p. 50.
11. Ibid., p. 51.
12. National Council on Alcoholism, *Facts on Alcoholism*, New York, 1983.
13. National Council on Alcoholism, *Alcohol in the Nation Is. . . .* New York.
14. *Facts on Alcoholism.*
15. *Alcohol in the Nation Is. . . .*
16. National Council on Alcoholism, Prevention and Education Department, *Facts on Teenaged Drinking and Driving*, 1982.

Chapter 8. A Loss of Absolutes

1. Alexis de Tocqueville, *Democracy in America*, vol. 1, in W. Cleon Skousen, *The 5,000 Year Leap* (Salt Lake City, 1981), pp. 81–85.
2. Ibid., p. 319.
3. The Lincoln Library of Social Studies, vol. 3 (Buffalo: Frontier Press, 1968), p. 949.
4. Marshall Foster and Mary-Elaine Swanson, "What Your History Books Never Told You," in *The American Covenant: The Untold Story* (West Lake Village, CA: Mayflower Institute, 1981), pp. 20–32.
5. "Schools Get 'F' in Character Building," *U.S. News & World Report*, December 3, 1984.

6. National Center for Health Statistics and News Reports, January 1985.
7. "A Nasty New Epidemic," *Newsweek*, February 4, 1985, p. 72.
8. De Tocqueville, p. 316.

Chapter 9. When Conservatives Aren't Conservative

1. Dan Carmichael, "Milk—America's Most Political Food (A Blend of Policies, Power and Money)," United Press International, June 1982.
2. Ibid.

Chapter 10. Creating Jobs in Japan

1. Sandy Harrison, "Domino Theory," *Ti-Caro Views* (Gastonia, N.C.: Ti-Caro, Inc., 1983), p. 2.

Chapter 11. The Disarming of America

1. "Probing the Press," *ON*, vol. 1, no. 3, p. 17.
2. Robert Rhodes James, ed., *Winston S. Churchill: His Complete Speeches 1897–1963*, vol. 2 (New York and London: Chelsea House Publishers, 1974), p. 7287.
3. Richard Nixon, *The Real War* (New York: Warner Books, 1980), p. 156.

Chapter 12. Facing the Realities of the Soviet Empire

1. John H. Davis, *The Kennedys: Dynasty and Disaster, 1848–1983* (New York: McGraw-Hill, 1984), p. 372.
2. Ray Bonds, ed., *The Vietnam War* (New York: Crown Publishers, 1979), p. 12.
3. Davis, p. 375.
4. Davis, p. 375.
5. Davis, p. 376.
6. Lyndon B. Johnson, *The Vantage Point* (New York: Holt, Rinehart & Winston, 1971), pp. 192–97.
7. "Capitalism Comes to the City," *Time*, October 29, 1984, p. 47.
8. V. I. Lenin, *Selected Works of V. I. Lenin*, in Louis F. Budenz,

The Techniques of Communism (Chicago: Henry Regnery Co., 1954), p. 66.

9. Ibid.

10. V. I. Lenin, *Selected Works of V. I. Lenin* (New York: International Publishers, 1971), p. 613.

Chapter 13. An American Strategic Foreign Policy

1. Richard Nixon, *The Real War* (New York: Warner Books, 1980), p. 168.

2. Nixon, p. 169.

3. Richard Halloran, "Europe Called Main U.S. Arms Cost," *New York Times,* July 20, 1984, p. A2.

4. Ibid.

Epilogue: The Courage of a Conservative

1. William Manchester, *American Caesar* (Boston: Little, Brown & Co., 1978), p. 398.

INDEX

INDEX